What Keynes Means

A Critical Clarification of the Economic Theories of John Maynard Keynes

by

Anatol Murad

Graduate Department of Economics
University of Puerto Rico

COLLEGE & UNIVERSITY PRESS · *Publishers*
NEW HAVEN, CONN.

Preface

The purpose of this book is to explain the principal ideas and theories of John Maynard Keynes. In writing it I have tried to emulate Adam Smith who was "always willing to run some hazard of being tedious in order to be sure that I am perspicuous." My aim was not to "simplify" the subject by skipping the difficult parts (though I did simplify it by omitting all those parts of the Keynesian theory which seemed to me unessential to an understanding of the principal ideas); nor was it my aim to write an "entertaining" book. The compulsion, currently prevalent in economics, to write entertainingly, is often pursued at the expense of clarity and preciseness. But surely such writing is as much out of place in economics as it is in other sciences—for instance biology and mathematics—where it is not the practice to write entertainingly. Presumably someone who reads a book on mathematics or biology—or on Keynes—wants to be informed about the subject, not entertained. Bearing this in mind, my only aim was to present my subject as clearly as I could.

It was clarification of the principal ideas and theories of Keynes that I had in mind in writing *What Keynes Means*, rather than any particular group of readers. The book should recommend itself to any and all who want to know and understand what the most famous economist of our age taught. I believe that *What Keynes Means* will be useful as a supplementary text for undergraduate and graduate classes in general economics and in economic theory; that it will prove helpful to advanced students preparing for examinations, as well as to teachers who wish to review the work of Keynes with the aid of a brief summary; and that it will answer the purpose of non-economists who want to learn about Keynes without being plunged into a maze of technicalities, but who want more substantial fare than is dished out by "popular" presentations of the subject.

To find out what an author has to say, it is usually best to read his own works; and all those who want to make a thorough study of Keynes must, obviously, read Keynes's own works, especially *The General Theory of Employment, Interest and Money*,[1] in which he set forth what has come to be known as the Keynesian theory. But as a first introduction to the subject, the *General Theory*[2] is not to be recommended. It makes difficult reading because, in many places, it is ambiguous and contradictory and consequently confusing.

Keynes himself did not intend the *General Theory* for non-professional students of economics. He addressed the book to his "fellow economists." While he hoped that it would be intelligible to others, he was primarily out to convert professional economists to his views. To achieve this, he apparently thought it necessary to express his ideas, which he said were really extremely simple and obvious, in the esoteric fashion dear to professional theoretical economists. To make his case convincing to his fellow economists, he made it unintelligible to the uninitiated. And even the professionals, impressed though they may be by Keynes's "rigorous" (usually meaning "mathematical") analysis, must find the *General Theory* difficult to understand, not to say incomprehensible, because of its ambiguities and contradictions. Perhaps this is the reason why relatively few people nowadays read the *General Theory* despite the fact that Keynesian ideas are enjoying greater popularity than ever before.

Students of Keynes customarily rely on commentaries and interpretations to pilot them through the *General Theory*. Among these are *Introduction to the Theory of Employment* by Joan Robinson, *The Economics of John Maynard Keynes* by Dudley Dillard, and *A Guide to Keynes* by Alvin H. Hansen.[3] In some

1. For full title, place and date of publication, etc., of every work mentioned in this book, see *List of Works Mentioned in this Book*, p. 217

2. In accordance with custom, this abbreviated designation of *The General Theory of Employment, Interest and Money* will be used. Numbers appearing in parentheses in the text of this book, as for instance on page 1, refer to pages in the *General Theory*.

3. A recent book, *The Failure of the New Economics* by Henry Hazlitt, although devoted exclusively to the *General Theory*, is not an elucidation, but an attempted point-by-point refutation of this work. This too could

respects these books parallel my own; each being devoted to the same objective as this book, that is, to make Keynes clear where he himself was obscure. But there are of course also many differences. I have given special attention to aspects of Keynes's economics left as unclear in the current literature as they are in the *General Theory*, particularly the theory of aggregate demand and the theory of interest. I have tried to unravel the ambiguities and contradictions of these theories and to restate them more intelligibly.

It has become customary in presentations of Keynesian theory to use certain simple diagrams.[4] A few such diagrams are included in this book, in part to clarify points under discussion, as is presumably always the purpose of using diagrams; but in part also to analyze and criticize the diagrams themselves and to point out the errors of Keynesian theory which they perpetuate.

The book is arranged as follows: Chapter I explains the place of Keynes in economics and the significance of his contribution; Chapters II-VII state the essentials of the Keynesian theory; Chapters VIII-XVII take up some aspects of Keynes's theories in greater detail and also point out some inconsistencies and contradictions in these theories; Chapter XVIII summarizes the innovations introduced by Keynes into economics. The headings of the remaining chapters are self-explanatory. They all have a bearing on whát Keynes means and should help to explain and clarify his ideas and theories.

What Keynes Means grew out of ten lectures I gave as a Fulbright lecturer at the University of Münster in 1958. Discussion with students in Germany and in the United States persuaded me that a brief book explaining in a fundamental way the main concepts and features of Keynes's theory would help them in their struggle with ideas which seem clear only at a distance and when shrouded in haze, but which become hazy when brought into a nearer and clearer light.

be useful, if it were not for the author's evident hostility to Keynes which vitiates his analysis.

4. Keynes himself used none of these diagrams. He had no predilection for relying on diagrams. In the *General Theory* he used only one diagram to illustrate a point in the theory of interest.

Contents

I	The Prophet of the New Economics	13
II	The Determinants of Employment	20
III	Aggregate Demand and Aggregate Supply	28
IV	The Theory of Consumption	35
V	The Theory of Investment	43
VI	Investment and Income	50
VII	Summary of the General Theory	56
VIII	Ambiguities and Contradictions in the Keynesian Theory of Aggregate Demand	59
IX	The Consumption Function	68
X	Saving	78
XI	The Multiplier	83
XII	Saving Equals Investment	96
XIII	Saving is Determined by Investment	102
XIV	Wages and Employment	114
XV	The Theory of Interest	127
XVI	Criticism of Keynes's Theory of Interest	141
XVII	The Theory of Money and Prices	153
XVIII	The Keynesian "Revolution"	167
XIX	Economic Policies Suggested by Keynes	175
XX	Evaluation and Criticism of the General Theory	187
XXI	The Principal Works of Keynes	197
XXII	Life and Character of John Maynard Keynes	207
	Chronology of the Life of J. M. Keynes	215
	List of Works Mentioned in this Book	217
	Index	220

List of Tables

1. Schedule of Aggregate Supply and
   Aggregate Demand   24

2. Consumption Schedule   37

3. Relation between Income, Consumption, and
   Investment   51

4. Relation between Income, Saving, and Investment   54

5. Multiplier Effect—Expansion   86

6. Multiplier Effect—Contraction   87

7. Multiplier Effect of Increase in
   Rate of Investment   89

8. Liquidity Preference Schedule   130

List of Diagrams

1. Relation between Aggregate Supply,
   Aggregate Demand, and Employment 30

2. The Consumption Function 38

3. Consumption Function (Showing C increasing
   proportionally less than Y) 41

4. Relation between Consumption,
   Investment, and Income 52

5. Relation between Saving, Investment, and Income 55

6. Relation between Real Wages and Employment 115

7. Liquidity Preference Function
   (Demand for media of payment) 131

8. L_1 Function (Transactions demand for
   media of payment) 133

9. L_2 Function (Hoarding demand for
   media of payment) 135

10. Determination of Rate of Interest by Interaction of
    Demand for Media of Payment (composed of L_1
    $+ L_2$) and Supply of Media of Payment 136

11. I Function and Family of S Functions 149

12. (A and B) Effects of Changes in Effective Demand
    on Output and Price Level 163, 164

Chapter One

The Prophet of the New Economics

John Maynard Keynes (1883-1946), was the chief architect of what has come to be known as the "new economics" or "Keynesian economics." There were of course many others who helped to form the new economics; but Keynes was the dominant figure among them. His influence on present-day economic thinking was greater than that of any other man in our century. He was the Einstein of economics.

KEYNES IN THE SUCCESSION OF FAMED BRITISH ECONOMISTS

Keynes is the most recent in a line of famed British economists who may be regarded as the prophets who formulated the economic doctrines and dominated the economic thinking of their respective epochs. Each of these prophets had his distinctive doctrine, though they shared certain basic ideas.

Adam Smith (1723-1790; *Wealth of Nations,* 1776), the first in the line, was champion of the principle of "let alone" or *laissez-faire*—"the obvious and simple system of natural liberty." *Laissez-faire* was to be the solution of society's economic problems and the assurance of the largest possible wealth of the nation.

David Ricardo (1772-1823; *Principles of Political Economy and Taxation,* 1817), formulated the "natural laws" governing value and the distribution of wealth and income. A pessimist, where Smith had been an optimist, Ricardo pointed to the physical limits to production, expressed in the "law of diminishing returns."

John Stuart Mill (1806-1873; *Principles of Political Economy,* 1848), while accepting Ricardo's "immutable" natural laws in so far as they applied to production, proclaimed that the laws of distribution could be changed by society.

Alfred Marshall (1842-1924; *Principles of Economics,* 1890), introduced the concept of equilibrium (e.g., equilibrium of demand and supply) which still dominates economic thinking. Like Mill before him, Marshall largely accepted the ideas of Ricardo, but tempered them with the optimism of the late Victorian period. Marshall was the teacher of Keynes.

Today Keynes occupies the position of pre-eminence previously held by this succession of famous predecessors. The influence of his ideas on our thinking has continued to grow even after his death. As yet, no new prophet has risen to take his place.

NATIONAL CHARACTER OF ECONOMICS

All these famous economists were British. This is explained partly by the fact that they were the propounders of *British* economics. Unlike the natural sciences, which are unaffected by national boundaries and national interests, economics has a strongly national character. Economic systems and problems vary from country to country and economic thinking consequently varies too. A German or a French list of economic prophets would undoubtedly add German names (Friedrich List, Gustav Schmoller) and French names (François Quesnay, Jean B. Say, Antoine Cournot) or substitute them for some in our list. But in part the British nationality of the prophets of economics is also explained by the fact that economics has been predominantly a British science. Even a German or French list would have to include a preponderance of British names. This is so largely because industrial capitalism matured in Britain before it did in other countries and because Britain was long the leading economic power. During this period the interpreters of the British economic system which set the pace for the rest of the world were British. A tradition for the cultivation of economic science grew up in Britain.

CLASS CHARACTER OF ECONOMICS

In addition to having been British, the prophets of whom Keynes is the most recent share another characteristic: they were the prophets of *capitalistic* economics. They expounded or defended or assumed the superiority of the system of private enterprise for profit. In addition to its national character, economics also has a class character. Economics may be, for instance, capitalistic economics or working-class economics, each leading to conclusions at odds with those of the other. This is why labor economists rarely see eye to eye with the economists of the National Association of Manufacturers; and why economists in capitalistic countries rarely agree with communistic economists. The capitalistic economists listed above, and their followers, are variously referred to as the "traditional" or "orthodox" or "classical" economists.

Of course there were also non-capitalistic, or anti-capitalistic prophets, notably Karl Marx. But Marx and his precursors and followers do not count in the capitalistic world; they belong to an "underworld," to use Keynes's expression, and appear to capitalists only as horned devils. "Orthodox" economists generally paid no attention to these devils or dismissed them with a few disdainful remarks.[1]

Keynes, then, was in the line of succession of British capitalistic economists. He followed, in most respects, the traditional, orthodox economics. Like every one of his famous predecessors, however, he departed from the received doctrine in some respects. The great innovation of Keynes was that he assigned the leading role in economics to *demand*. The significant obstacles to production, Keynes argued, do not come from the limitations to supply, i.e., from "diminishing returns," but from

1. Referring to Marx and Engels (co-author, with Marx, of the *Communist Manifesto* and other writings) Keynes wrote: ". . . they invented a certain method of carrying on and a vile manner of writing, both of which their successors have maintained with fidelity. But if you tell me that they discovered a clue to the economic riddle, still I am beaten–I can discover nothing but out-of-date controversialising." (Letter to G. B. Shaw, quoted in Harrod, *The Life of John Maynard Keynes*, p. 462.)

insufficient demand. In this he contradicted the received ortho-
doxy and laid the foundation for the "new" economics.

ECONOMICS AND IDEOLOGY

Keynes and his famous predecessors have been referred to as
"prophets." This was intended to stress the ideological character
of economics. Every "system" of economics savors of a religion, a
system of dogmas, an ideology. It is said that discussions of the
Keynesian theory in its early days had the quality of revival
meetings. The same can surely be said of discussions of Marxian
theory and of other systems of economics. They are like religions,
each having its own prophets. The Keynesian doctrine, too,
was a new religion. Keynes was its prophet. (To adherents of
other economic religions he is, of course, a false prophet.)

The comparison of economics with religion should not be
understood to mean that economics is nothing more than a set
of beliefs, an ideology. Economics is partly ideology, partly
argument for policy, and partly science—in that order of importance, when regarded from the standpoint of its significance
to society.

In their capacity as scientists, economists describe and explain what people do, how they organize the production and
use of wealth. But a mere factual recital of, let us say, the
consumption habits of people in given income groups or of
factors determining plant location is not likely to cause much
excitement or get much attention.

What economists have to say is more likely to get a hearing
if it can be used as a basis for policy. Every policy must rest on
some theory. Free traders and protectionists, those who favor a
balanced budget and those who are for deficit spending, income
tax advocates and sales tax advocates, high wage and low
wage champions—all bolster their policies with one or another
economic theory. An economic theory which cannot be used
to formulate and prescribe economic policies will not get much
attention, no matter how valid it may be scientifically.

But what is even more important than its usefulness as a
basis for policy, is the ideological appeal of an economic theory.

To win followers, an economic doctrine must arouse fervor and fire the imagination. Adam Smith's "obvious and simple system of natural liberty" was inscribed on the banner of the capitalists. Workers could rally to the Marxian call to overthrow capitalistic exploitation. Such ideas have nothing to do with science. They are rather religious. Salvation comes through *laissez-faire,* or through socialism, depending on your faith.

The ideology embodied in a particular economic theory expresses the interests and aspirations of particular groups—of merchants, for instance, or of manufacturers, or of wage workers. It is their credo. It gives those groups a respectable, scientific-sounding justification for pursuing their own advantage.

All the famous works in economics have a strongly ideological hue; and it is chiefly this which accounts for their fame. This should not be taken to imply that the authors of those works were mere propagandists or that they deliberately colored the truth for the sake of pleading a cause. Though we can of course never know what a person really thinks, we may assume that the prophets of economics were honestly seeking the truth and to report the truth as they saw it. It is not that they played false tunes, but that the ideological overtones turned out to be the more significant and lasting elements of their music.

Like other systems of economics, that of J. M. Keynes contains a mixture of the three elements: science, policy, and ideology.

Some of the importance of Keynes's work consists in his having shed new light on the behavior of a capitalistic economy, especially in industrially advanced countries.

Of more obvious significance, however, are the policy implications of Keynes's economics. All his active life Keynes was concerned with getting certain policies adopted by the British and other governments, and his writings were really arguments for these policies. He wanted the government to intervene in order to remedy what he considered the worst fault of the capitalistic system: instability. To overcome this instability Keynes recommended all sorts of schemes, from the gold exchange standard to compulsory saving. Present-day economic policy in the United States and elsewhere leans heavily on Keynesian theory.

But if policy was uppermost in Keynes's mind, his system of economics derives perhaps even greater significance from its ideological overtones. Keynes was the prophet of what might be called "state capitalism"—that phase of capitalism in which the state must intervene to keep the economy going. His advocacy of state intervention in the economy did not make Keynes a socialist, as some diehard *laissez-faire* adherents charged. On the contrary, Keynes had no use for socialism. He championed private enterprise, but he opposed *laissez-faire*. Whereas the classical economists had argued that the state must keep "hands off" the economy in order to give free rein to private enterprise, Keynes recognized that, in his time, private enterprise needed state intervention and support in order to survive. His ideal was an economic system of private enterprise run for profit, but with the state responsible for maintaining stability and full employment. Even as 150 years earlier Adam Smith had been the prophet of *laissez-faire* capitalism, so now Keynes was hailed as a prophet by "New Dealers" and other nonsocialistic advocates of national economic planning who detected in his theories a justification for their respective systems of intervention in the economy of the nation.

THE "KEYNESIAN REVOLUTION"

At the time he was working on the *General Theory,* Keynes wrote: "I believe myself to be writing a book on economic theory which will largely *revolutionise* . . . the way the world thinks about economic problems."[2]

The expression "Keynesian Revolution" is not infrequently used in reference to the work of Keynes.[3] But it should not be thought that Keynes was a revolutionist in the sense of one who wants to overthrow the existing order of society. Quite on the contrary, he wanted to save it. He was a revolutionist only in the sense that he wanted to change "the way the world

2. Letter to G. B. Shaw, quoted in Harrod, *op. cit.,* p. 462. (Italics mine.)
3. *The Keynesian Revolution* is also the title of a book by Lawrence R. Klein, 1947.

thinks about economic problems," as he said. Nevertheless there is a connection between the revolution in thought and a real economic revolution. The revolution in thought is a reflection of the revolutionary change that had taken place in the economy of society. Capitalism had reached a new stage of development. Old theories were no longer meaningful. New theories had to be developed. Keynes developed such a new theory. What this revolutionary theory of Keynes is will be explained in the following chapters.

Chapter Two

The Determinants of Employment

THE PROBLEM OF UNEMPLOYMENT

Keynes set out to discover what determines the volume of employment. Why are jobs so scarce at times that one third or more of the working population is unemployed, as it was in the United States in 1932? Why, at other times, are jobs so plentiful that employers cannot find enough people to fill them? And why, as a rule, is there at least a moderate amount of unemployment? What, in short, accounts for the fluctuations in the volume of employment from which countries with a private enterprise system characteristically suffer?

Types of unemployment

Unemployment can be voluntary or involuntary. When a person does not want to work because he does not need any income from working, or because the wages offered him are not high enough, he is voluntarily unemployed. Voluntary unemployment hardly poses a problem. It is when people are involuntarily unemployed, when they want and need jobs but are unable to get them even though they are willing to work for less than the prevailing wages, that a problem exists. When we speak of unemployment, we usually have in mind *involuntary* unemployment. It is only in this sense that the term unemployment is used in this book.

Economists customarily distinguish three different types of unemployment: structural, frictional, and cyclical or depression unemployment.

Structural unemployment is attributable to the "structure" of the economy. Such unemployment is often found in the so-called "underdeveloped" countries which are predominantly agricultural. If there are more workers than can be employed in agriculture, these extra workers may remain unemployed for lack of factories where they could be put to work.

Frictional unemployment results from frictions in the functioning of the economy. When workers change jobs, for instance, it usually takes them some time before they find new jobs. In the meantime they are unemployed. When a plant is shut down for installation of new machinery, workers may be out of work for days or weeks. Strikes, too, account for frictional unemployment.

Cyclical or depression unemployment reflects the cyclical fluctuations of the economy—the ups and downs of prosperity and depression.

It is only this third type of unemployment that Keynes dealt with. He wanted to find out how cyclical unemployment comes about; what determines cyclical fluctuations in the volume of employment.

KEYNES'S ASSUMPTIONS

In developing a theory to supply answers to these questions Keynes assumed that, in the short run, the quantity and quality of labor and of productive equipment, technology, the organization of economic life, and the tastes and habits of people remain unchanged. Of course they do change; and in the long view these changes are of great significance. But Keynes was primarily concerned with the short run; and in the short run, over the span of a few months or even a few years, changes of this type are generally small enough to justify neglecting them while searching out the more significant determinants of fluctuations in employment.

Another assumption is that we are dealing with a "closed economy," meaning an economy which has no external relations, such as foreign trade. This assumption is of course dropped in all those parts of the analysis which do deal with external relations.

Keynes further assumed a private enterprise economy in which workers are employed only by business firms[1] in quest of profit. In actual fact not only business firms but also all sorts of non-profit organizations and especially governments employ labor; and the determinants of such non-profit employment are quite different from the determinants of employment offered by business firms. Keynes, however, wanted to discover what causes this latter, quantitatively most important, type of employment to be unstable.

Other assumptions made by Keynes will be noted when the topics to which they are relevant come up for discussion.

OUTPUT, EMPLOYMENT, AND INCOME

The quantity of employment which firms will offer at any given time depends directly on the quantity of output they decide to produce. A greater output can be produced only with more labor, a smaller output requires less labor. In other words, output and employment rise and fall together.

Since the volume of employment depends on the decisions of firms to produce given quantities of output, the question: what determines employment? is the same as the question: what determines output? Keynes's theory, therefore, is not only a theory of employment; it is also a theory of the determinants of output as a whole. Furthermore, the community's total output being the same thing as its real income, and the money value of output being the same thing as the money income of the community, the Keynesian theory may also be regarded as a theory of the determinants of income as a whole.

OUTPUT MEASURED BY EMPLOYMENT

To explain fluctuations in the quantity of output it is necessary to have some way of expressing and measuring this quantity. How can output be measured?

It would not be possible to measure output by adding up the

---

1. Keynes used the term *entrepreneur,* meaning enterpriser. The term *firm* is here used as a shorter, as well as a more familiar designation for the organizations—individual proprietorships, partnerships, and corporations —which direct production and employ people.

physical quantities of goods produced; there is no way of getting a meaningful total by adding spinach to speedometers. To measure output by adding up the dollar values of these various products involves all the well-nigh insoluble difficulties of constructing price indexes. The only unambiguous way to define the quantity of output, said Keynes, is in terms of the labor required to produce it. This would not hold for the long run, because in the long run the quantity of output produced by a given quantity of labor can and does change considerably. But in the short run, with techniques of production assumed to be unchanging, a greater quantity of goods can be produced only by the employment of a correspondingly greater (though not numerically proportional) quantity of labor; and we can use the quantity of labor employed as a measure of the quantity of output produced.

DEMAND AND SUPPLY DETERMINE OUTPUT

On what basis do firms decide what output to produce and, therefore, what quantity of labor to employ? They decide, said Keynes, on the basis of their *expectations* as to what volume of output will yield them the greatest profit. These profit expectations, in turn, depend, on the one hand, on the costs which largely determine the amounts of money for which firms are *willing* to sell various quantities of output; and, on the other hand, on the amounts of money for which they expect to be *able* to sell these same quantities of output. To put it differently, the volume of output which firms decide to produce depends on *aggregate demand* and *aggregate supply*.

AGGREGATE DEMAND AND AGGREGATE SUPPLY

Aggregate demand is defined as the schedule of the aggregate sums of money which firms expect the community to be willing to pay for goods at each possible level of output and corresponding income and employment. The word *schedule* needs special attention. Aggregate demand is not any particular amount of money: it is the whole schedule of such amounts of

money which firms expect to be offered for various quantities
of output. The particular aggregate sum of money the community is expected to be willing to pay for goods when output
is at a given level is the "aggregate demand price" of that
output; it is the same as the gross income, or the "proceeds,"
resulting from this output and the corresponding employment.

Aggregate supply is similarly defined as the schedule relating
aggregate supply prices to the corresponding quantities of output and employment. The aggregate supply price of a given
output is the minimum sum of money for which firms are
willing to sell this output. Unless firms believe their proceeds
from the output will be at least that much, they will not produce
this output.

The relation between aggregate demand and aggregate supply
is illustrated in Table 1.

Several simplifying assumptions have been made in this
illustration. One assumption is that all workers are equally
productive. A skilled worker who produces twice as much as
an unskilled worker would be counted as two workers. Another
assumption is that wage rates are constant, so that the cost
of employing 50 million workers is exactly double that of em-

TABLE 1

Schedules of Aggregate Supply and Aggregate Demand

N^2	Z	D
Quantity of labor employed to produce various quantities of output (O) (millions of workers)	Aggregate Supply prices (annual rate, in billions of dollars of constant value)	Aggregate demand prices, or proceeds (annual rate, in billions of dollars of constant value)
0	0	150
25	150	225
50	300	300
75	450	375

2. The letters designating quantity of labor employed, aggregate supply
and aggregate demand, or proceeds, are the ones chosen by Keynes. One
may wonder why he did not use L for labor and S for supply. The reason
is probably that he had already assigned the letter L to liquidity (see
Ch. XV, p. 127 below) and S to saving.

ploying 25 million workers. It is further assumed that there are not more than 75 million workers. If all these are employed, "full employment" prevails.

According to the values assumed in Table 1 for employment (N), aggregate supply (Z), and aggregate demand (D), firms expect the community to spend at the annual rate of 150 million dollars even if firms produce nothing at all and the community consequently has no current income and will have to draw on past accumulations. The community would be expected to spend 225 billion dollars when firms employ 25 million workers to produce an output costing 150 billion dollars; the community again being willing to draw on past accumulations to supplement current income. If, on the other hand, firms were to produce an output requiring the employment of 75 million workers, they would have to sell this output for not less than 450 billion dollars in order to cover their costs and normal profit;[3] but they would expect to be able to sell it for only 375 billion dollars, because at this level of output and income the community would be unwilling to spend as much as its entire income.

As long as aggregate demand exceeds aggregate supply, the expectation of larger than normal profits would lead firms, in competition with each other, to expand output. But when aggregate supply exceeds aggregate demand, firms expect less than normal profits; and finding it unprofitable to produce so large an output, they curtail output and employment.

On our assumptions, the output which turns out to be the

---

3. Since we are dealing here with the costs of all firms taken together, we must exclude from costs all those payments which firms make to each other, such as, for instance, the cost of materials which one firm buys from another. What is left are the so-called factor costs, i.e., the wages, rent, and interest which firms pay out to people who furnish the so-called *factors of production*—labor, natural resources, capital. Keynes tended to regard labor as the only real factor of production and therefore tended to identify factor costs with wages.

The *normal profit* which must be added to those factor costs is the minimum amount of profit which firms expect to make if they produce a given output.

most profitable for firms, and which competition will lead them to produce, is an output requiring the employment of 50 million workers. Firms will offer this output for 300 billion dollars; and 300 billion dollars, just enough to cover their costs and normal profit, is exactly what they expect to receive for it. This output is called the "equilibrium" output. If firms produce exactly this quantity of output, they have no incentive either to expand or contract output.

CHANGES IN AGGREGATE DEMAND AND AGGREGATE SUPPLY

A change in aggregate demand means that firms expect the community to be willing to spend more (or less) dollars for given quantities of output than they expected it to be willing to spend before. A change in aggregate supply means that firms are willing to sell given quantities of output for more (or less) dollars than before.

If either aggregate demand or aggregate supply should change, equilibrium output and employment would change, too.

The causes and effects of changes in aggregate demand are the main subject of the *General Theory* and will be examined in subsequent chapters.

Changes in aggregate supply could be caused by changes in the technical conditions of production which affect the *real* costs of production. These changes Keynes assumed to be negligible in the short run.[4] Another reason for changes in aggregate supply is that *money* costs of production may change. If money wages and other costs should be cut by, let us say, one-half, firms might be willing to cut prices by one-half. But if money wages and other *costs* fall by one-half, money *incomes* also fall by one-half, since what is cost to firms is income to those who receive the payments. Wages, for instance, are costs to employers, income to employees. With its money income reduced by one-half, the community's aggregate demand would fall proportionately. As a result, employment, output, and *real*

4. See p. 21, above.

income would remain unchanged, though prices and *money incomes* would have dropped to half their former levels.[5]

Since we are primarily concerned with finding out what determines employment and *real* income, i.e., the output of goods, aggregate demand and aggregate supply, shown in Table 1, are expressed in dollars of constant value, which means that a given sum of money measures an unchanging quantity of goods and of real income.[6]

For the reasons stated above, aggregate supply, understood to mean the amounts of dollars of constant value for which firms are willing to sell various quantities of output, is not likely to change much in the short run. Keynes assumed it to be unchanging.

EMPLOYMENT DETERMINED BY AGGREGATE DEMAND

With aggregate supply unchanging in the short run, *the volume of output, employment, and income is determined by aggregate demand. This is the central proposition of Keynes's theory of employment.*

---

5. At least this will be the general tendency. The effects of wage reductions on employment will be more fully discussed in Chapter XIV, below.

6. This, however, can be done only for values of Z and D at less than and up to full employment. Beyond full employment, the *real* income of the community cannot rise further, but its *money* income can continue to rise. A rise in money income not accompanied by a rise in real income must, of course, drive prices up. The assumption of a constant dollar, i.e., of stable prices, must therefore be dropped when conditions beyond *full employment* are considered.

Chapter Three

Aggregate Demand and Aggregate Supply

In the present chapter the concepts of aggregate demand and aggregate supply, introduced in Chapter II, are further analyzed. Attention is called to the difference between these concepts and the ordinary concepts of demand and supply. Certain features of aggregate demand and aggregate supply are elucidated with the aid of a diagram.

DIFFERENCES BETWEEN KEYNESIAN AND ORDINARY CONCEPTS OF DEMAND AND SUPPLY

Demand and supply are ordinarily defined as schedules relating the quantities of goods demanded or supplied to various prices. For example, the demand for butter (in a specified market at a specified time) is such that at $1.00 per pound, 100 pounds would be bought: at 50¢—1000 pounds; at 25¢—2000 pounds; and so on. The demand for butter is the entire schedule showing the various quantities of butter demanded at various prices. The supply of butter, correspondingly, is the schedule showing the various quantities of butter offered for sale at various prices.

These concepts of demand and supply differ from the Keynesian *aggregate* demand and *aggregate* supply in several respects:

1. Ordinary demand and supply relate quantities of commodities to *per unit prices* of these commodities. Aggregate demand and aggregate supply relate *aggregate expenditures* on commodities to the output of these commodities (measured by the quantity of labor employed to produce this output). This is one reason for the adjective *aggregate*.

2. Ordinary demand and supply relate prices to quantities of *commodities*. Aggregate demand and aggregate supply relate expenditures to quantities of *output* and *employment*.

3. Ordinary demand and supply refer to a *particular commodity*. Aggregate demand and aggregate supply refer to the *aggregate output of all commodities* (measured by the quantity of labor employed to produce it). This is a second reason for the adjective *aggregate*.

In view of these differences it is necessary, when referring to demand and supply, always to indicate in which of the two senses the terms are used. In many situations one sense applies, in many other situations the other sense applies. Keynes himself did not always use demand and supply in the sense of aggregate demand and aggregate supply. To avoid confusion, therefore and at the risk of tediousness, the adjective *aggregate* should always be added when demand and supply are used in this sense. When ordinary demand and supply are referred to, this can be indicated either by using no qualifying adjective or by speaking of *price demand* and *price supply*.

AGGREGATE DEMAND AND AGGREGATE SUPPLY SHOWN GRAPHICALLY

The schedules of aggregate demand and aggregate supply assumed in Table 1 are shown graphically in Diagram 1. The horizontal axis is the employment axis. A scale along this axis indicates all possible levels of employment (N) from zero to 75 million workers. The vertical axis is the aggregate demand (D) and aggregate supply (Z) axis (not to be confused with the slanted D and Z lines). The scale along this axis indicates dollar amounts of aggregate demand prices or proceeds (D) and of aggregate supply prices (Z) from zero to 450 billion dollars.

The supply price of a zero output is zero dollars. This relationship is expressed by the point O—the "point of origin"—which marks the intersection of the two axes. The aggregate supply price of an output produced by 25 million workers is 150 billion dollars. This relationship is shown by the point A in

Z, D Axis
   Z (Aggregate supply) and
   D (Aggregate demand) Annual
      rate, in billions of dollars of constant value

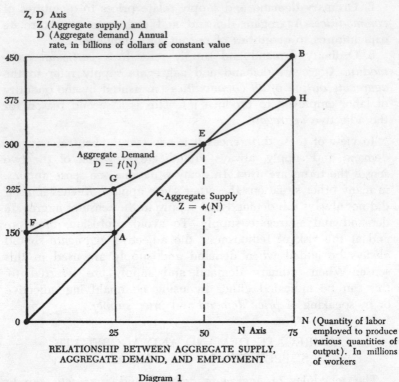

RELATIONSHIP BETWEEN AGGREGATE SUPPLY,
AGGREGATE DEMAND, AND EMPLOYMENT

Diagram 1

which a vertical line (ordinate) rising from the point marked
25 along the N axis intersects a horizontal line (abscissa)
starting from the point marked 150 on the Z, D axis. Points E
and B show the other values of Z and N assumed in Table 1.
If there were points showing the aggregate supply price for
every quantity of output and employment, there would be so
many points that they would look like a line. The slanted line
connecting the four Z points shown in the diagram may be taken
to be this line; it shows the value of Z for every possible value
of N between zero and 75 million workers. This line is called
the *aggregate supply line* or the *aggregate supply function* or
the *Z line*.

The *aggregate demand line,* or *aggregate demand function,* or *D line* is similarly derived by connecting the points F, G, E, H, which show the relation between the values of D and N assumed in Table 1. The aggregate demand line shows the proceeds accruing to firms from the quantities of output produced by every possible number of workers from zero to 75 million.

THE AGGREGATE SUPPLY FUNCTION

In the preceding section the Z and D lines were referred to as *functions.* A function is "a magnitude so related to another magnitude that to values of the latter there correspond values of the former."[1] The aggregate supply schedule (Table 1) shows that Z (aggregate supply price) depends on N (quantity of labor employed); therefore Z is said to be a function of N; it is called the *aggregate supply function* and is expressed by the equation $Z = \phi(N)$. In Diagram 1, the functional relationship between Z and N is expressed by the Z line. The Z line, therefore, is also referred to as the *aggregate supply function,* since it is the graphic expression of $Z = \phi(N)$.

Since the Z line shows the relationship between two variable magnitudes, or *variables,* Z and N, one could as well call this line the N line, and the functional relationship shown by it, the N function, i.e., the employment function. The reason why it is not called the employment function, but the aggregate supply function, is that it is customarily the *dependent* variable which is regarded as a function of the *independent* variable. Z (aggregate supply price) is the *dependent* variable, while I (employment) is the *independent* variable. How much the aggregate supply price will be depends on how much is being produced, i.e., on how many people are employed, not the other way around.

Several properties of the Z line shown in Diagram I need comment:

Lineality. The Z line in Diagram 1 is shown as a straight line

1. *Webster's New International Dictionary,* 1939 edition, p. 1019.

because wages (including other factor costs) plus normal profit are assumed to be constant per worker employed and therefore directly proportional to the number of workers employed. The aggregate supply price of an output produced by two workers must, on this assumption, be twice as great as the aggregate supply price of the output of one worker, half as great as the aggregate supply price of the output of four workers, and so on.

Origin. The Z line must start at the point of origin, O, because if firms should employ no labor at all, and therefore produce nothing at all, their output would cost them nothing; the supply price of zero output would therefore be zero.

Inclination. Although the Z line must start at the point of origin, it need not be inclined at a 45° angle, as it is shown to be in Diagram 1. This inclination is merely the result of the choice of scales along the two axes. If, for instance, the intervals on the N axis were made twice as large, so that an inch would represent only 12.5 million workers instead of 25 million workers, while the scale along the vertical axis remained unchanged, the Z line would rise at an angle of only about 25°. Nevertheless, the choice of a scale which will produce a 45° Z line is deliberate. In the next chapter we shall deal with other 45° lines which despite their different names are in fact the same as the Z line. Since these other lines are inclined at 45°, it would be confusing to show the Z line inclined at any other angle.

THE AGGREGATE DEMAND FUNCTION

The aggregate demand schedule (Table 1) shows that D (proceeds) depends on N (quantity of labor employed). D, therefore, is a function of N. It is called the *aggregate demand function.* This designation is used also for the D line (Diagram 1) which is a graphic representation of the aggregate demand function.

It was shown earlier that Z—aggregate supply—is also a function of N. The D function, however, is not identical with the Z function. The values of D corresponding to the various values of N are different from the corresponding values of Z, except where the D and Z lines intersect. To differentiate the aggregate demand function from the aggregate supply function $(Z = \phi(N))$, Keynes wrote the aggregate demand function $D = f(N)$.

Analysis of the D line will be the subject of the next two chapters. At this juncture it should be noted only that the D line in Diagram 1 is a straight line merely because it was simpler to assume it to be straight; unlike the Z line, it does not originate in O because even with no employment whatever people will want some goods; and, for reasons to be explained in the next chapter, the D line must rise less steeply than the Z line, so that these two lines must intersect at some point.

EFFECTIVE DEMAND

The quantity of output that is actually produced, and the corresponding level of employment and income, are given by the intersection of the Z and D lines (Diagram 1). In our example those lines intersect at a point corresponding to 300 billion dollars and 50 million workers. The value of D, where D is intersected by Z, Keynes called *effective demand*.[2]

Effective demand is not a *schedule* of aggregate expenditures, as is aggregate demand; it is a *particular amount of aggregate expenditures*; it could just as well be called *aggregate expenditures* or *proceeds*. Being the same thing as aggregate expenditures, effective demand must also be the same thing as aggregate income. What the community spends on goods is what the firms take in. What the firms take in, they partly pay out in wages and other factor costs; the rest is their profit. Factor costs are factor incomes. Factor incomes plus profit are aggregate income. Therefore, aggregate expenditures equal aggregate income; therefore, effective demand equals aggregate income.

2. Keynes used the symbol D for effective demand, but it is preferable to designate it by the letter E (following Professor Dillard, *The Economics of John Maynard Keynes*) in order to avoid confusing effective demand with the aggregate demand function, as Keynes himself occasionally did.

EQUILIBRIUM OF AGGREGATE DEMAND AND AGGREGATE SUPPLY

The intersection of the D and Z lines also indicates the equilibrium position of the economy. In our example, equilibrium would mean aggregate expenditures of 300 billion dollars and employment of 50 million workers. It should be noted that this is not *full employment*. On our assumptions, full employment would prevail if 75 million workers were employed. This larger number would be employed only if the D line intersected the Z line in point D. As long as the D and Z lines are as in Diagram 1, the economy will be in equilibrium at less than full employment.

This is an important conclusion of Keynes's theory. It contradicts the classical economists who maintained that equilibrium necessarily entailed full employment. They argued that as long as there were unemployed people willing to work for wages corresponding to their productivity, aggregate supply would increase, and output and employment expand, until full employment was reached. In terms of our diagram, the classical argument was that the Z line would be lowered until it intersects the D line at point H. How Keynes countered this argument was already touched upon (pages 26-27), but will be more fully explained in Chapter XIV.

Chapter Four

The Theory of Consumption

Since Keynes regarded aggregate demand as the short-run determinant of employment, output, and income, he devoted his attention chiefly to the analysis of aggregate demand. In fact, the *General Theory* may be regarded as a theory of aggregate demand. The general outlines of this theory are presented in this and the three following chapters. Certain ambiguities and contradictions in the Keynesian theory of aggregate demand which the reader may detect in this presentation will be cleared up in Chapter VIII.

The theory of aggregate demand explains the position and shape of the aggregate demand function; it tells us what determines the aggregate expenditures the community is ready to make at various levels of income.

Aggregate expenditures may be conveniently separated into two components: 1) consumption expenditures, and 2) investment expenditures. The present chapter deals with consumption expenditures and the theory of consumption. The theory of investment will be taken up in Chapter V.

CONSUMPTION EXPENDITURES AND CONSUMPTION

Consumption expenditures include not only actual cash outlays for consumption goods, but also purchases of consumption goods made on credit (e.g., installment purchases) and consumption goods received by people as "payment in kind" of all or part of their wages, as for instance the use of a house given to a minister or a college professor as part of his salary.

In view of these qualifications it appears that we are not really dealing with consumption *expenditures*. Why, then, not speak simply of *consumption*? Because we are not dealing with *consumption*, either. Consumption takes place when people use goods to satisfy wants. We consume our food not when we buy it, but when we eat it—which may be much later. We consume our clothes, furniture, automobiles over considerable periods and long after we bought them and paid for them. For purposes of our analysis it is not the consuming of these goods, but the buying them and paying for them, that matters. Therefore, the emphasis on consumption *expenditures* rather than on consumption itself. In the following discussion, however, the word *consumption* is often used for short, in the implied though somewhat inaccurate sense of consumption *expenditures*.

THE PROPENSITY TO CONSUME

Consumption expenditures depend on what Keynes called the *propensity to consume*, which means the disposition of the community to consume a given proportion of its income. People are so constituted that the larger their income, the smaller will be the proportion of it which they consume, and the larger the proportion which they save. People with the smallest incomes often consume more than their income—by dipping into reserves or by borrowing or by living on charity. On the other end of the scale, the multimillionaire consumes but a small part of his income even when he splurges.

For the community as a whole the same general relationship holds, at least in the short run: if the community's income is low, consumption may exceed income, at some higher level of income, consumption will be equal to income; and at still higher levels of income, consumption will increasingly fall short of income.

Keynes held that if a person's (or a community's) income increases merely because prices rise, he will want to consume just as great a part of it as when his income was smaller, but prices correspondingly lower. In other words, mere changes in *money income* are not likely to change the proportion of income consumed. It is the *real income* which matters. The propensity to consume expresses the relation between consumption and *real* income.

THE CONSUMPTION FUNCTION

The relation between consumption (C) and the amount of income (Y) may be illustrated by the following hypothetical consumption schedule, showing in Column C what aggregate consumption expenditures would be if income were as shown in Column Y.

The consumption schedule shows that the amount of consumption depends on the level of income. Consumption is a function of income; this function is called the *consumption function*. Keynes expressed the consumption function by the equation $C = \chi(Y)$.[1] The consumption function is graphically illustrated by the C line in Diagram 2.

The psychological attitudes which account for the community's propensity to consume will be discussed in Chapter X. For the moment we shall center our attention on clarifying the meaning of the consumption function and of the diagram illustrating it.

TABLE 2

Consumption Schedule
(annual rates, in billions of dollars
of constant value)

Y	C
0	100
50	125
100	150
150	175
200	200
250	225
300	250
350	275
400	300
450	325

1. It is also expressed as $C = C(Y)$. Cf. Kurihara, *Introduction to Keynesian Dynamics;* Hansen, *A Guide to Keynes*.

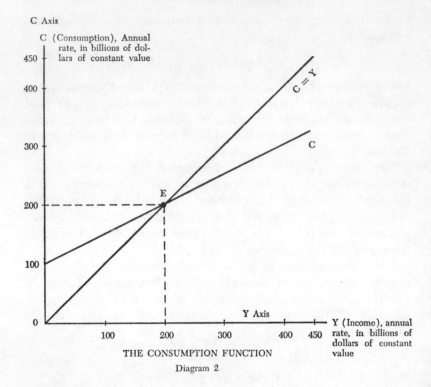

THE CONSUMPTION FUNCTION

Diagram 2

The income line

The line labeled C = Y in Diagram 2 is drawn in order to bring out more clearly the relation of consumption to income. The (C = Y) line shows what the consumption function or consumption line would look like if the community consumed its entire income and saved no part of it, regardless of the level of income. If income were zero, consumption would be zero; if income were 50, consumption would be 50; if income were 100, consumption would be 100, and so on. Consumption is assumed to be equal to income, no matter how large income may be. If the same scale is used along both axes, the (C = Y) line must be a straight line rising to the right, from the point of origin, at a 45° angle.

Because the (C = Y) line shows what the relation between

C and Y would be if the community never saved any part of its income, it is sometimes called the *zero-saving function*. It could also be called the *income line,* for if every point on this line shows consumption equal to income, then every point on this line must also show income. Indeed this line is the *income* line under all circumstances, regardless of what the consumption function may be; it is the *consumption* line only in the hypothetical and improbable case of consumption being equal to income for all values of income.[2]

Relation of income line to consumption line

The 45° income line in Diagram 2 helps to bring out more clearly the characteristics of the consumption function (C) which reflects the fact that people do save. The C line is above the (C = Y) line for income lower than 200 billion dollars. This shows that at low incomes people consume more than their incomes and consequently *dis*save; when income is 200 billion dollars, they neither save nor dissave (on the figures

2. If the 45° line is the income line it could also be regarded as the aggregate supply function or Z line. The Z line, it will be remembered, shows the minimum dollar amounts which firms must expect to recover from selling any possible output, if they are to produce this output. How much is this minimum dollar amount which firms must expect to recover? It is as much as the dollar value of the output. Firms will produce a given output if they expect to get back for it a dollar amount equal to the value (i.e., factor cost plus normal profit) of what they produce; the dollar value of output is the community's money income, even as the output itself constitutes the community's real income. It follows that for every quantity of labor employed, the income produced by this quantity of labor is the aggregate supply price of the output.

If the horizontal scale in Diagram 1 were changed from output (measured in number of workers employed) to dollars (measuring cost of output plus normal profit) the Z line would be the same as the income or (C = Y) line, or 45° line. This is why the Z line in Diagram 1 was shown as a 45° line, exactly like the (C = Y) line in Diagram 2. It should be observed, however, that the 45° inclination of these lines is a result of the choice of scales along both axes. (See Chapter III, p. 32.) In Diagram 2 both axes have dollar scales and it is reasonable to make the intervals the same on both axes. If this is done the (C = Y) line must be a 45° line. If the intervals used along one axis were different from those on the other axis, the (C = Y) line would of course not be a 45° line.

assumed in Table 2); for incomes above this figure, the C line is lower than the 45° line, showing that people save increasing amounts of their incomes.

Properties of the consumption function

Three features of the consumption function require comment:

1. As income rises, consumption rises too, but not by as much as income. This is why the slope of the C line is less than that of the (C = Y) line. Keynes referred to this feature of the consumption function as the *psychological law of consumption*. This law is basic to the Keynesian theory. It is the principal explanation of why aggregate demand is not automatically sufficient to absorb all possible quantities of output.

2. The C line starts above the point of origin. At low levels of income the community wants to consume more than its income. Even if there is no income, people must consume if they are to live. The Keynesian theory would hold just as well, however, if the consumption function started at the point of origin. Its essential feature is that it rises less steeply than the 45° line.

3. The C line is not necessarily straight. It is here assumed to be straight only to simplify the exposition. On the assumption of a linear consumption function the community always increases its consumption by a fixed proportion of increments in its income. In our example, consumption expenditures increase by 25 dollars for every 50-dollar increase in income. Actually, it is probable that consumption increases not only absolutely less, but also proportionally less, than income, so that every 50-dollar increase in income would be accompanied by a steadily decreasing increment in consumption—such as 25 dollars, 20 dollars, 15 dollars, and so on. A consumption line depicting this situation would be a curve tending to flatten out for high values of income, as shown in Diagram 3.

Changes in the propensity to consume

People may decide to consume a larger or smaller portion of their incomes. When their propensity to consume increases, i.e., when they consume a larger portion of their income at any

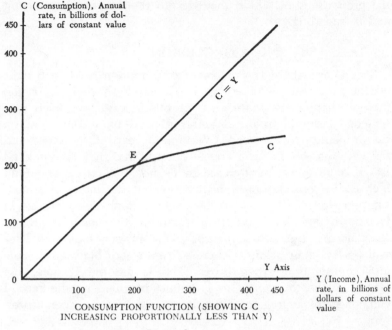

CONSUMPTION FUNCTION (SHOWING C
INCREASING PROPORTIONALLY LESS THAN Y)

Diagram 3

given level of income, the C line would be shifted upward. A decrease in the propensity to consume means a downward shift of the C line.

Changes in the propensity to consume must not be confused with changes in consumption expenditures themselves. An increase in consumption expenditures may be the result of an increase in income, the propensity to consume remaining unchanged. Movements along the C line are not the same as movements of the C line itself.

Reasons for shifts in the propensity to consume will be discussed in Chapter IX, on the Consumption Function. Experience indicates that the propensity to consume is fairly stable in the short run. At any rate Keynes regarded it as practically stable. It will be remembered that he assumed habits and tastes to be unchanging in the short run, and this includes the habits of people regarding the disposition they make of their incomes—the proportions in which they devote their incomes to saving and to spending.

CONCLUSION

Several aspects of the theory of consumption needing further clarification will be taken up in Chapters IX and X. In the present chapter the main ideas of this theory have been presented. Consumption expenditures depend on income and on the propensity to consume. Consumption expenditures rise and fall with income. But the crucial point is that they rise and fall *less* than income. An increase in income will bring about an increase in consumption expenditures, but the increase in consumption expenditures will be smaller than the increase in income. At low levels of income, consumption may be greater than income. But as income rises, consumption sooner or later will be less than income. There will be a gap between income and consumption expenditures. The larger the income, the larger will be the gap. This gap must be filled by the second component of aggregate expenditures: investment expenditures.

Chapter Five

The Theory of Investment

Aggregate demand is the schedule of aggregate expenditures corresponding to various levels of output and employment. These expenditures are the sum of consumption expenditures and investment expenditures. The preceding chapter explained the determinants of consumption expenditures. The present chapter deals with investment expenditures and the determinants of the volume of investment expenditures.

THE MEANING OF INVESTMENT

Definition of investment

In ordinary everyday language the term *investment* means the purchase of any income-yielding asset, such as securities (stocks and bonds), or real estate. The assets themselves are also referred to as investments. In the language of the financial world the term *investment* is used in the narrower sense of *securities*. But in the language of economic theory investment has a different meaning; it means expenditures for additions to capital. Capital is usually defined as man-made goods used in production, such as machines and other productive equipment. Keynes, accordingly, defined investment as the "addition to the value of the capital equipment which has resulted from the productive activity of the period." (62)[1] According to this definition, securities are not an investment. Nor is the purchase of securities an investment, although it may have an indirect

1. Numbers appearing in parentheses in the text refer to pages in the *General Theory*.

connection with investment. Only expenditures for new capital equipment which has "resulted from the productive activity of the period" constitute *investment*.

The term *capital equipment* in the above definition is somewhat vague. Presumably it means production equipment, such as machines and buildings. Capital, however, includes not only machines and buildings, but also inventories. Investment, then, means expenditures for currently produced production equipment and inventories. Since all goods currently produced must be either currently consumed or added to production equipment or to inventories, investment can also be defined as expenditures for all that portion of current output which is not currently consumed.

Investment expenditures and investment

Investment expenditures must be understood to include not only actual cash outlays for capital equipment, but all purchases of capital equipment (always including inventories) made on credit. Also included in investment expenditures must be the value of all capital equipment which, instead of being purchased, is produced by firms for their own use.

In view of these qualifications it might appear preferable not to use the expression investment *expenditures,* but to refer simply to *investment.* The term *investment* is in fact used throughout this book as a synonym for investment *expenditures.* The reason why any emphasis at all is put on the aspect of investment as *expenditures* is that the Keynesian theory envisages output and employment as being determined by the receipts which firms expect from various levels of output; the receipts of firms are the same thing as the expenditures made for the purchase of the output; and these expenditures are the sum of consumption *expenditures* and investment *expenditures.*

Investment expenditures are made only by firms

Production is carried on by firms. Production equipment, or capital equipment, consequently is bought only by firms. This means that investment expenditures, being expenditures for capital equipment, are made only by firms. Purchase of a machine by an individual for his private use, and not for use in producing goods for sale, would be counted as a consumption expenditure; and the machine would be regarded as a consumption good.

Since only firms make expenditures for capital equipment, firms making capital equipment can sell their output only to other firms. All firms taken together, then, do not really sell the capital equipment they produce and do not really receive any payment for this capital equipment. Firms taken together receive payment for only that part of their aggregate output which is sold to consumers. The part of aggregate output which is not sold to consumers is retained by firms (taken together) as additions to their capital equipment; and the value of the unsold portion of output is the "addition to the value of the capital equipment" which Keynes defined as investment.[2]

DETERMINANTS OF INVESTMENT

On what does the volume of investment depend? Keynes said that it depends on 1) the *marginal*[3] *efficiency of capital* and 2) the *rate of interest*.

2. To speak of *value* in this connection is inaccurate because there may be changes in the value of capital equipment which are not due to the "productive activity of the period." By the end of the period prices may have risen and made capital equipment, including the portion of it produced during the period, more valuable. What really matters is not the addition to the value of capital equipment, but the costs incurred in the process of adding to the capital equipment. We should, therefore, define investment as costs incurred in the process of adding to capital equipment. This definition does not contradict the definition of investment as expenditures for capital equipment. The incurring of costs is in most cases associated with expenditures and for practical purposes we may equate costs with expenditures.

3. The word "marginal" in economics means "on the borderline." Thus "marginal utility" is the utility added to the total utility of a stock of goods by the addition of one unit of the good; the "marginal cost" is the addition to total cost occasioned by the production of one additional unit of output. Or: the "marginal buyer" is the buyer least anxious to buy a good at the prevailing price; "marginal land" is the land only barely worth using.

The marginal efficiency of capital

Keynes defined the marginal efficiency of capital as the *rate of discount* which equates the returns expected from an additional capital asset during its life with the supply price of that asset. To illustrate: a firm buys a machine for $1000. The machine is expected to last only one year, after which it can be sold as scrap for $200. During its one year of service the machine is expected to yield a return of $900. The marginal efficiency of the machine is that rate of discount which will equate the $1100 the firm expects to have got out of the machine by the end of the year ($900 + $200 salvage) with the $1000 it has to pay for it now. According to the formula

$$\text{Cost} = \frac{\text{Expected return} + \text{Salvage value}}{1 + \text{Rate of discount}} \quad \text{or}$$

$$\$1000 = \frac{\$900 + \$200}{1 + r}$$

the marginal efficiency (r) of the machine is 10 per cent.

To take another illustration: a capital asset costing $1000 and expected to yield $100 a year indefinitely or for a long time, such as 50 or 60 years, would have a marginal efficiency of (approximately) 10 per cent.[4]

Differently stated, the marginal efficiency of capital is the profit, expressed as a rate of return on investment, expected from the last increment of capital. The emphasis here must be on the word *expected*. What businessmen *expect* future profits to be depends on their state of mind. This state of mind is subject to sudden great changes in response to a multitude of factors some of which have nothing to do with the business situation.

---

4. $\text{Cost} = \dfrac{R_1}{1 + r} + \dfrac{R_2}{(1 + r)^2} + \dfrac{R_3}{(1 + r)^3} \cdots + \dfrac{R_n}{(1 + r)^n}$

R stands for expected returns in year 1, year 2, year 3, . . . year n of the expected life of the asset. r stands for marginal efficiency of capital. These symbols were not those used by Keynes himself, but by Hansen in *A Guide to Keynes*.

As a result, the marginal efficiency of capital is highly unstable; and this leads to sudden and wide fluctuations in investment.

The rate of interest

The rate of interest is the price paid for the use of media of payment, also variously called *funds* or *cash* or *money*.[5]

How high or low the rate of interest is at any time depends on the quantity of media of payment and on the liquidity preference of the community. Liquidity preference is the desire of people to hold media of payment, the most liquid form of wealth, in preference to interest yielding assets (debts). Other things being equal, a strong liquidity preference will cause interest rates to be high; owners of media of payment are then willing to lend them to others only if they get a higher interest rate than they would be willing to take if their liquidity preference were weaker; and borrowers will have to pay these higher rates of interest if they want to get media of payment.

A fuller discussion of the Keynesian theory of interest must

5. As a rule Keynes used the terms *cash, funds,* and *money* as synonyms and assumed that money is co-extensive with *bank deposits* (167), but he did not do so invariably. The use of these several terms in economic literature is unfortunately not uniform, often contradictory, and almost always confusing. A chief cause of confusion is the failure to distinguish between media of payment and monetary units; between the dollar as an expression of value and the dollar bill or dollar coin.

To avoid ambiguity and confusion, the following terminology is used throughout the rest of this book:

1. Coin, note currency (e.g., Federal Reserve notes, silver certificates), and deposit currency (i.e., demand deposit obligations of commercial banks) are collectively referred to as *media of payment.*

2. The words *cash* and *funds* are not used except when reference is made to the use of these terms by Keynes or other economists, and in firmly established phrases, such as "cash balances theory" or "cash transactions theory" or "loanable funds theory."

3. The word *money* is used only in such contexts as "money wages," "money incomes," where *money* does not refer to media of payment, but to monetary units, such as dollar, franc, pound sterling. The word *money* is not used in the sense of *media of payment,* except again when reference is made to its use by Keynes or others. In these cases I have put the word *money* in quotation marks or in other ways indicated to the reader that the use of the word is someone else's and not my own.

be postponed to later chapters. Here it is necessary only to point to the connection between the rate of interest and investment. Investment will be pushed to the point at which the marginal efficiency of capital equals the rate of interest. If the marginal efficiency of capital is 10 per cent and the rate of interest is 5 per cent, it would pay to borrow at 5 per cent in order to acquire capital assets expected to yield a return of 10 per cent. Firms would therefore be encouraged to invest more. The larger the volume of investment, however, the higher would the supply prices of capital assets be driven and the lower would be the expected return, so that the marginal efficiency of capital would fall until it is brought to equality with the rate of interest. When the marginal efficiency of capital falls below the prevailing rate of interest, further investment will cease. It will not be profitable for firms to borrow media of payment in order to invest; and firms owning media of payment will find it more advantageous to lend them out at interest than to use them to buy capital equipment.

A lower rate of interest will tend, other things remaining unchanged, to stimulate investment; a higher rate, to discourage investment. This does not mean, however, that the level of investment could be regulated at will, and be held at the full employment level, through the manipulation of interest rates. In depression, when profit expectations collapse, i.e., when the marginal efficiency of capital falls to zero or below zero, even a zero rate of interest will not induce firms to expand their productive facilities or their inventories. On the other hand, when profit expectations are at prosperity peaks, even a high rate of interest may not dampen the firms' enthusiasm for capital expansion.

Autonomous and induced investment

The preceding analysis of the determinants of investment shows that according to Keynes, investment, unlike consumption, does not depend on the level of income. Investment is not a function of income and employment. Investment is an independent, or *autonomous*, variable. More correctly, it is independent of income; it depends on other things—on the marginal efficiency of capital and on the rate of interest.

The view that investment is autonomous overlooks the fact that, to a considerable extent, investment depends on the level of consumption. If consumption increases, firms need more capital in order to expand the output of consumption goods. Investment induced by increases in consumption is called *induced investment*.

Since consumption varies with income, investment induced by consumption also varies with income. Induced investment, therefore, in a function of income and employment.

The effect which increases in consumption, and therefore increases in income, have on investment is known as the *acceleration effect*.[6]

Keynes assumed that increases in consumption are short-lived and that producers have unused productive capacity which can be drawn into use to supply temporary increases in consumer demand. On these assumptions there would be no induced investment and the acceleration effect would be inoperative.

INVESTMENT HIGHLY VARIABLE

Whereas consumption, the first component of aggregate demand, is relatively stable, investment, the second component, is highly unstable. The volume of investment is subject to great variation, reflecting the ups and downs in profit expectations of firms. It is investment, therefore, which in the last analysis accounts for fluctuations in aggregate demand and, consequently, for fluctuations in output, employment, and income.

The relation of investment to aggregate demand and to output, employment and income will form the subject of the next chapter.

6. See pp. 94-95.

Chapter Six

Investment and Income

Keynes regarded investment as the unstable element in aggregate demand. He attributed the instability of the capitalistic economy primarily to the instability and volatility of investment. A change in the volume of investment, he argued, will be reflected on a magnified scale in output, employment and income. The present chapter shows how this comes about.

INVESTMENT FILLS THE GAP BETWEEN CONSUMPTION AND AGGREGATE EXPENDITURES

The aggregate expenditures of the community are always the sum of consumption expenditures and investments. With a given consumption function, the level of aggregate expenditures—and therefore the level of income, output and employment—depends on investment expenditures.

Consumption, it will be recalled, increases less than income (or aggregate expenditures), so that as income increases there is a widening gap between income (or aggregate expenditures) and consumption expenditures. This gap must be filled by investment expenditures, the second component of income and expenditures. Turning again to Table 2,[1] it will be seen that if there were no investment at all, income (Y) would have to be 200 billion dollars, a figure just equal to consumption. Income could rise to 250 billion dollars only if there were investments of 25 billion dollars. This amount of investment would be necessary to fill the gap between a 250 billion dollar income and the 225 billion dollars of consumption corresponding to this income.

1. P. 37.

To have income rise to 400 billion dollars would require 100 billion dollars of investment.

On the other hand, income would fall below 200 billion dollars only if investment were negative. Thus, income would fall to 100 billion dollars if the community were to *dis*invest 50 billion dollars; in that case, it would be consuming part of its capital or be living at the expense of foreign communities.

Whatever the level of income, Y, it is always equal to C + I. The gap—positive or negative—between income and consumption must always be filled by (positive or negative) investment. Investment is the decisive element which, given the propensity to consume, determines what the level of income, and of consumption, will be.

RELATION OF INVESTMENT TO INCOME

The relation between investment and income may be clarified with the help of another example with hypothetical figures. Table 3 shows what income (Y) would be, given the figures for consumption (C) assumed in Table 2, and assuming investment (I) is, in the first case, 25 billion dollars, and in the second case, 50 billion dollars. (All these magnitudes are to be understood as representing annual rates; e.g., consumption is

TABLE 3

Relation Between Income (Y), Consumption (C),
and Investment (I), annual rates,
in billions of dollars of constant value

Case 1					Case 2			
Y	C	I_1	$C + I_1$		Y	C	I_2	$C + I_2$
100	150	25	175		100	150	50	200
150	175	25	200		150	175	50	225
200	200	25	225		200	200	50	250
250	225	25	250		250	225	50	275
300	250	25	275		300	250	50	300
350	275	25	300		350	275	50	325
400	300	25	325		400	300	50	350
450	325	25	350		450	325	50	375

at the *rate* of so and so many dollars a year.) In Diagram 4, the figures are translated into lines.

In both cases, 1 and 2, investment (I) is shown as being the same for all values of income (Y), because I, unlike C, is assumed to be independent of Y.[2] On this assumption the I line in Diagram 4 must be a horizontal line—no matter what the level of income may be, investment is always the same; and the (C + I) line, representing aggregate expenditures, must be parallel to the C line, because it is nothing but the C line to which a constant value has been added throughout. The 45° line is here designated as Y = C + I because all points on this line show the equality of income with consumption plus

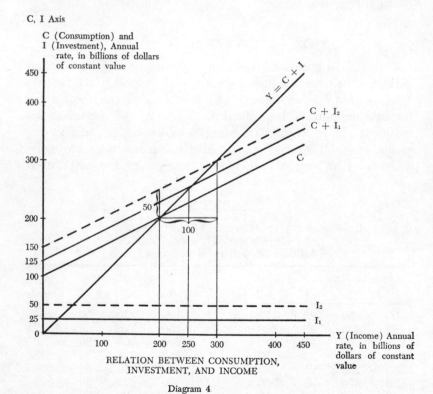

RELATION BETWEEN CONSUMPTION, INVESTMENT, AND INCOME

Diagram 4

2. See pp. 48-49.

investment.[3] Since the actually realized income (Y) must by definition always equal consumption plus investment (C + I), the actually realized Y will be given by the intersection of the (C + I) line with the income line—the 45° line. Thus, on the figures assumed here, if investment is zero, income must be 200 billion dollars, because the C line intersects the 45° line at a point corresponding to 200 billion dollars; if I is 25 billion dollars, Y must be 250 billion dollars, corresponding to the intersection of the (C + I₁) line with the 45° line; and if I is 50 billion dollars, Y must be 300 billion dollars, as shown by the intersection of the (C + I₂) line with the 45° line.

THE MULTIPLIER

A change in investment, consequently, is associated with a multiple change in income. The relation between changes in income and the changes in investment which bring them about, is expressed by the *multiplier*. In the illustration used above the multiplier is 2, since a change in investment produces a change in income twice as great—a 25 billion dollar increase in I being associated with a 50 billion dollar increase in Y. The multiplier applies also in reverse, a decline in I leading to a greater decline in Y, assuming that other things remain unchanged.

The multiplier shows clearly how changes in investment can produce larger changes in income. In the example above, the multiplier is low because the community was assumed to devote only one half of every increase in income to consumption. Thus, when Y increases by 50 billion dollars, C increases by only 25 billion dollars. If the proportion of additional Y consumed were larger, the multiplier would be larger, too. For instance, if people consumed four-fifths, or 80 cents, of every additional income dollar, the multiplier would be 5; a 25-dollar increase in investment would raise income by 125 dollars, of which four-fifths, or 100 dollars, would be spent on consumption. The multiplier will be analyzed more fully in Chapter XI.

3. See pp. 38-39.

SAVING AND INVESTMENT

The level of income, as we have seen, is determined by total expenditures, i.e., by the sum of consumption and investment. An alternative way of showing the determinants of income is to relate investment to saving. The relation between income and saving and investment is shown in Table 4 and Diagram 5.

For every level of income, saving is the difference between income and the portion of income which is consumed. Thus, on the basis of the figures assumed in Tables 3 and 4, if income is 200 billion dollars, saving must be zero, because the entire income is consumed; if income is less than 200 billion dollars, saving will be negative because the community consumes more than its income; as income rises above 200 billion dollars, saving will become steadily greater.

Saving is what was earlier referred to as the "gap" between income and consumption. This gap must be filled by investment, since total income must always be equal to consumption plus investment. If the amounts invested should be smaller than the saving gap, income would have to shrink to a level at which the gap would be reduced to the size of current investment expenditures; if investment were larger than the gap, then income would have to rise to a level at which the saving gap

TABLE 4

Relation Between Income (Y), Saving (S),
and Investment (I), annual rates
in billions of dollars of constant value

Y	S	I
100	-50	50
150	-25	50
200	0	50
250	25	50
300	50	50
350	75	50
400	100	50
450	125	50

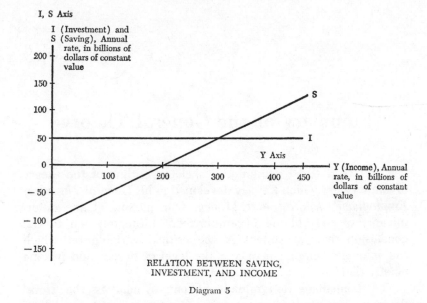

RELATION BETWEEN SAVING,
INVESTMENT, AND INCOME

Diagram 5

is large enough to absorb investment. In Diagram 5, therefore, the level of income is determined by the intersection of the I and S lines. Only at that point is investment just sufficient to fill the expenditure gap caused by saving. If less were invested, income would have to fall to the level at which correspondingly less would be saved; and if more were invested, income would rise until it reached the level at which the community wants to save an amount equal to investment.

The relation between saving and investment will be analyzed in greater detail in Chapters XII and XIII.

Chapter Seven

Summary of the General Theory

Chapters II to VI presented a skeleton outline of the theory of employment which Keynes developed in his *General Theory of Employment, Interest and Money*. Our pursuit of the determinants of the volume of employment ultimately led to the conclusion that investment is the critical variable on which the volume of employment and the level of output and income chiefly depend.

The immediate determinant of employment is the firms' decisions to produce a certain quantity of output. These decisions are based on aggregate supply and aggregate demand. The conditions on which firms are willing to supply goods are unlikely to change much in the short run. With a given aggregate supply function it is aggregate demand which determines the volume of output and employment.

Aggregate demand, or aggregate expenditures, are made up of two components, consumption and investment. Consumption depends on the level of income and on the propensity to consume. The propensity to consume tends to be fairly stable in the short run. The unstable element in aggregate expenditures is investment. Fluctuations in investment are the chief cause of fluctuations in employment and income. A low volume of investment will keep the community's income low. Income cannot rise unless investment rises (assuming the propensity to consume to be unchanged); and if investment does rise (or fall), income rises (or falls) by a multiple of investment.

Rich countries like the United States tend to have a low propensity to consume and must therefore rely on a high level of investment to keep income at or near the full employment

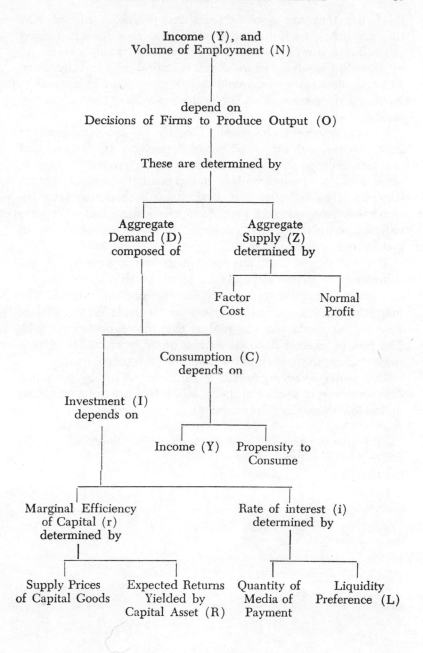

level. But they are also industrialized, which is indeed why they are rich; already having much capital, they have increasing difficulty in finding opportunities for additional investment. As a result, the advanced industrial countries tend to suffer from a chronic deficiency of demand and from consequent unemployment and depression. This is the dilemma for which a solution must be found.

Keynes developed his theory largely in order to discover how a country can be pulled out of depression. He showed that it is necessary in such cases to increase the propensity to consume and to strengthen the inducement to invest.[1] Poorer countries, paradoxically, may be better off than rich ones because they have a higher propensity to consume and a stronger inducement to invest and consequently have less difficulty in maintaining full employment.

The investment decisions on which the prosperity of the community so largely depends are based partly on the marginal efficiency of capital and partly on the rate of interest. The marginal efficiency of capital, in turn, depends on the cost of new capital goods and the returns they are expected to yield. The rate of interest depends on the quantity of media of payment and on the community's liquidity preference.

This sequence of arguments is summarized in the preceding diagram showing at the top the variables that are to be explained and below them their determinants.

1. The economic policies based on the Keynesian theory will be discussed in Chapter XIX.

Chapter Eight

Ambiguities and Contradictions in the Keynesian Theory of Aggregate Demand

The reader was warned earlier that some of the concepts and definitions used by Keynes in analyzing aggregate demand contain ambiguities and contradictions. To clear up these ambiguities and reconcile these contradictions it is necessary to reformulate some of the propositions of the Keynesian analysis.

SUBJECTIVE VERSUS OBJECTIVE AGGREGATE DEMAND

One of the difficulties in Keynes's analysis of aggregate demand stems from his definition of aggregate demand (D) as "the proceeds which entrepreneurs *expect* to receive from the employment of N men" (25, italics added). Keynes emphasized over and over again that it is the firms' expectations which constitute the aggregate demand on which they base their decisions to produce. Aggregate demand, D, he said, is composed of two parts, D_1 and D_2. D_1 is "the amount which the community is *expected* to spend on consumption," and D_2 is "the amount which it is *expected* to devote to new investment" (29, italics added).

This repeated emphasis on expectations would lead one to think that Keynes intended to call attention to the contrast between expectations and realizations—between what firms believe the community will spend and what it actually spends. But when he came to analyze aggregate demand more closely, he suddenly switched from the question of what determines the *expectations* of firms to an analysis of what determines *actual* expenditures. The aggregate demand function which started out as expressing proceeds expected by firms is suddenly converted into a function expressing the proceeds which firms actually realize at various levels of employment.

Are expected proceeds, then, the same as realized proceeds? If Keynes had intended to make these two magnitudes identical, he could have said so specifically. He did not say so, however. In fact he made specific reference to realized proceeds *not* being identical with expected proceeds. At one point, for example, Keynes wrote in the *General Theory*: "The *actually realized* results of the production and sale of output will only be relevant to employment in so far as they cause a modification of subsequent expectations" (47, Keynes's italics). And yet, in many other places, he identified aggregate demand with *realized* proceeds, although he had defined aggregate demand as *expected* proceeds.

There are, then, two concepts of aggregate demand in the Keynesian theory: *subjective* aggregate demand and *objective* aggregate demand. The *subjective* aggregate demand is the schedule of proceeds expected by businessmen who decide, on the basis of these expectations, how much to produce and how many people to employ. The *objective* aggregate demand is the schedule of expenditures actually made by the community at various levels of income and employment—regardless of the subjective expectations on the part of businessmen. Keynes never explained how these two concepts are related, in what ways the subjective aggregate demand or "expected proceeds function" is different from the objective aggregate demand or "realized proceeds function," or whether these two are identical.

AGGREGATE DEMAND REDEFINED

The way out of these contradictions is to define aggregate demand as the schedule of *actual* expenditures made by the community at various levels of income and employment; or, in other words, as the schedule of proceeds *realized* from various levels of income and employment.

This definition of aggregate demand in the *objective* sense, as *actual* proceeds, contradicts Keynes's definition of aggregate demand in the *subjective* sense, as "the proceeds which entre-

preneurs *expect to receive.*" Nevertheless, our redefinition of
aggregate demand is not inconsistent with Keynes's emphasis
on expectations as the crucial factor determining the current
volume of output and employment. These expectations, however,
instead of being themselves regarded as constituting the aggregate demand for goods, must be regarded as the businessmen's
estimates of what the aggregate demand for goods actually is.
That this was what Keynes really meant is indicated by his
statement that "the significance of . . . my . . . arguments lies
in their attempt to show that the volume of employment is
determined by the *estimates of effective demand* made by the
entrepreneurs . . ." (78, italics added).[1]

Of course the firms' estimates of aggregate demand are always
more or less wide of the mark. As firms discover that their
subjective estimates of actual, objective aggregate demand were
wrong, they adjust their decisions to produce accordingly. The
actually realized results of the production and sale of output
will cause modifications of subsequent expectations.

IS AGGREGATE DEMAND EQUAL TO
AGGREGATE SUPPLY?

There is another difficulty contained in the Keynesian aggregate demand analysis. Proceeds—whether in the sense of expected or realized proceeds—will supposedly equal the aggregate
supply price of output only in equilibrium, i.e., only at the point
at which the D and Z lines intersect. At all other levels of employment and output, D will be either below or above Z. (A
glance at Diagram 1 will be helpful.)

We have seen earlier that aggregate demand, D, is the same
thing as the sum of consumption, C, and investment, I; and that
aggregate supply is the same thing as income (the Z line is the
same as the 45° income line). To say that aggregate demand
equals aggregate supply only in equilibrium is, therefore,
equivalent to saying that C + I, or total expenditures, will

1. Effective demand, it should be remembered, is "the value of D, where
it is intersected by Z," or, in other words, the proceeds actually realized
—or is it the proceeds expected?—from actual output.

equal income only in equilibrium. This is what Diagram 4 showed, in conformity with the customary presentation of this subject.[2]

But this cannot be right. Income, Y, must by definition always be equal to C + I, regardless of whether or not income and employment are at the equilibrium level. C + I can never be greater or smaller than Y. The (C + I) line should, therefore, be identical with the (Y = C + I) line—the aggregate demand function should be identical with the aggregate supply function.[3]

This, however, would obviously be inconsistent with Keynes's principal idea. It would be a reassertion of "Say's law" which Keynes was out to disprove. Say's law or the "law of markets" is the law which asserts that aggregate demand is always equal to aggregate supply; that supply creates demand; that the only reason people produce is to create the means to satisfy their desire to consume and to pile up more capital goods. Keynes argued that this is not so; that aggregate demand falls short of aggregate supply because people save and because they want to accumulate, not capital goods, but media of payment.

INTENDED AND UNINTENDED
CONSUMPTION AND INVESTMENT

To rescue the Keynesian theory of aggregate demand from the contradiction which turns it into the opposite of what Keynes intended, a further modification of the theory is re-

2. Similar diagrams can be found in many textbooks on economics. See, for instance, Kurihara, *Introduction to Keynesian Dynamics*, p. 110 and elsewhere.

3. This objection does not apply to Diagrams 2 and 3 which show the relationship of consumption to income. C is not equal to Y at every level of Y. But C + I is.

Does the objection apply to the familiar demand and supply diagram? No, because this diagram shows only what quantities buyers stand ready to buy, and sellers stand ready to sell, at various prices. There is no contradiction in showing D and S lines crossing each other. It would be different if the two lines in such a diagram were to show quantities bought, and quantities sold, at various prices. In this case the lines would have to be identical, for at no price can the quantity sold be different from the quantity bought.

quired. A distinction must be made between actual consumption and investment, on the one hand, and intended or unintended consumption and investment on the other hand. Consumption, C, must, accordingly, be broken down into two component parts: C_i and C_u. C_i is the amount the community *intends* to consume at any given level of income, while C_u represents *un*intended consumption. Similarly investment, I, must be broken down into I_i—intended investment—and I_u unintended investment.

The community's propensity to consume may be such that it *intends* to consume at the rates assumed in tables 2 and 3: 300 billion dollars when income is 400 billion dollars, 150 billion dollars when income is 100 billion dollars, and so on. The consumption function, then, relates *intended* consumption to income; it should therefore be labeled C_i instead of C.

In most situations, what the community *intends* to consume at a given level of income may be what it actually does consume at that level of income. In any case, actual consumption could never be greater than intended consumption, as long as people cannot be forced to consume more than they want to consume. But actual consumption could be less than intended consumption. This could happen especially at low levels of income, when the community intends to consume more than its income, and consequently also more than its output. Thus, when only 100 billion dollars' worth of goods is being produced, the consumers, who want to have 150 billion dollars' worth of goods, may be thwarted by the unavailability of goods. But also at high levels of income shortages of goods may prevent people from consuming as much as they intend to consume. This is a familiar condition in wartime.

Of greater importance than the distinction between actual and intended consumption, is the distinction between actual and intended investment. Firms may intend to invest a certain amount, say 50 billion dollars, when income is 400 billion dollars (see Table 3, Case 2).[4] This means that if income were at that level, firms would be producing 400 billion dollars' worth of

4. P. 51.

goods and would expect to sell 350 billion dollars' worth of these goods to consumers. But, on the figures assumed in Table 3, consumers would spend only 300 billion dollars. Firms would therefore find themselves with 50 billion dollars' worth of goods unsold and unintentionally added to their inventories. Since additions to inventories constitute investment, this un-intended addition to inventories would represent unintended investment.

Whenever firms produce an output which is larger than what the community intends to absorb, the result will be unintended investment in the form of goods left unsold. Conversely, when firms produce less than what the community intends to absorb, stocks of goods will have to be drawn upon to satisfy consumer demand. This unintended reduction of inventories constitutes unintended *dis*investment.

Whereas unintended investment may be either positive or negative, unintended consumption, as pointed out above, can only be negative. Consumers may be forced by shortages of goods to consume less than they intended, but they cannot be made to consume more than they intended.

KEYNES ASSUMED THAT FIRMS ALWAYS PRODUCE EQUILIBRIUM OUTPUT

Keynes recognized the importance of unintended investment, i.e., of unintended accumulations and decumulations of in-ventories, for day to day business decisions (76). His failure to include unintended investments in his theory of aggregate demand stems from his assumption that the economy is always in equilibrium, i.e., that firms always correctly estimate effective demand. Since he defined effective demand as *proceeds expected by firms* (and not as expenditures intended by the community) he necessarily had to say that firms always produce the output which equals effective demand. There would be no reason for assuming that firms would ever produce anything but the amounts which they expect to be able to sell most advantageously. On Keynes's definition of effective demand as *expected* proceeds, firms always produce the equilibrium output. And in equilibrium there is no unintended consumption and investment.

We have seen that this subjective definition of effective demand—and of the aggregate demand function—contains difficulties which force its rejection in favor of the objective definition of aggregate demand as the schedule of the amounts the *community intends to spend*. With this redefinition of aggregate demand, the assumption that firms always hit upon the quantity of output which will correspond exactly to the effective demand is no longer tenable. And when firms do not produce the equilibrium output, actual expenditures must deviate from intended expenditures.

THE KEYNESIAN THEORY OF AGGREGATE DEMAND RESTATED

The Keynesian theory of aggregate demand can now be restated as follows:

1. The aggregate demand function, D, relates expenditures *intended by the community* to employment (or to income). It does not relate proceeds *expected by firms* to employment (or income).

2. The aggregate demand function is the sum of two components: the consumption function and the investment function.

The consumption function relates the amounts which the community *intends* to consume to employment (or to income).

The investment function relates the amounts which the community *intends* to invest to employment (or to income).

The aggregate demand function, therefore, shows what the community *intends* to consume and *intends* to invest; it does not show what firms *expect* consumption and investment to be, nor does it show the actual amounts of consumption and investment corresponding to every level of income and employment.

$$D = C_i + I_i. \text{ D is not } D_1 + D_2; \text{ nor is it } C + I.$$

3. Aggregate consumption, C, at every income level, is the sum of intended consumption, C_i, plus unintended consumption, C_u.

Aggregate investment, I, is the sum of intended investment, I_i, plus unintended investment, I_u.

4. No matter what output (and income) firms produce, it will always be equal to C + I. But only when income and employment are at the equilibrium level will C +I be equal to C_i + I_i; above the equilibrium level C_i + I_i falls short of C + I; below the equilibrium level C_i + I_i exceeds C + I.

5. Effective demand, E, is the point on the D = (C_i + I_i) function where it is intersected by the Z (or Y = C + I) function. Firms try to estimate the effective demand correctly and to produce an output which will be exactly equal to what the community intends to consume and invest.

6. Firms, however, rarely if ever estimate effective demand correctly. When they overestimate it, they will be left with goods unsold, representing unintended investment, I_u.

When firms underestimate effective demand, their inventories will be depleted. Firms will *dis*invest unintentionally; I_u will be negative. When firms underestimate effective demand, consumers' goods may not be available in sufficient quantities or varieties to satisfy consumer demand. Actual consumption, therefore, may be less than intended consumption. Unintended consumption, C_u, may be negative.

7. When firms overestimate effective demand and consequently find themselves making unintended investments in unsold goods, they will reduce output and employment. When firms underestimate effective demand and consequently disinvest as their inventories shrink, they will expand output and employment. Employment and output—and income—are thus continuously fluctuating, not only because effective demand fluctuates, but also because firms do not correctly estimate demand. Employment, output, and income are forever oscillating around the equilibrium level which is itself continuously shifting in response to changes in the amounts the community intends to consume and invest at various levels of income.

The reformulation of Keynes's theory of aggregate demand leaves the essentials of his theory of employment unchanged. As was shown in Chapters II-VII, Keynes argued that, with a given aggregate supply function, the level of employment, output and income is determined by effective demand, i.e., by aggregate expenditures. Aggregate expenditures consist of consumption expenditures and investment expenditures. The volume of consumption corresponding to a given income depends on the propensity to consume. The volume of investment depends on the marginal efficiency of capital in relation to the rate of interest.

The determinants of employment, output, and income are therefore:

1. the propensity to consume,
2. the marginal efficiency of capital, and
3. the rate of interest.

Chapter Nine

The Consumption Function

The main outlines of the theory of consumption were presented in Chapter IV. There the meaning of the propensity to consume and the consumption function were explained. The present chapter further clarifies some aspects of the "law of consumption," the propensity to consume, and the consumption function.

THE PSYCHOLOGICAL LAW OF CONSUMPTION

Keynes based his theory of consumption on what he called the "psychological law" that "men are disposed, as a rule and on an average, to increase their consumption as their income increases, but not by as much as the increase in their income" (96). The psychological law of consumption accounts for the general characteristics of the consumption function, introduced in Chapter IV; it explains the position and slope of the consumption line in Diagrams 2 and 3. The consumption function, in turn, determines the general characteristics of the aggregate demand function; and the aggregate demand function determines output, income and employment. Thus the psychological law is really the cornerstone of the Keynesian theory.

Whether this law is really a "psychological law" is questionable. Perhaps it is merely a mode of behavior to which men conform in a capitalistic society. That men do behave in this way in our society is, however, confirmed by statistical evidence and by experience. The proposition itself cannot be regarded as novel; it is rather self-evident. But the far-reaching implications of this proposition were by no means self-evident; they eluded most of the pre-Keynesian economists.

According to Keynes, the psychological law of consumption applies not only to real persons, but also to corporations and governments, even, in some connections, to the central government. Corporations and governments, too, tend to increase their expenditures by less than the increase in their incomes; they, too, save. Mostly, however, it was the consumers whom Keynes seems to have had in mind when he discussed the psychological law of consumption and the consumption function. And since in general he applied his analysis to the *private* sector of the economy, with a view to arguing the need for governmental intervention to correct the malfunctioning of private enterprise, Keynes could hardly have envisaged the central government as being subject in the same way to this "psychological law" as consumers, business firms, and local governments.

AVERAGE AND MARGINAL PROPENSITY TO CONSUME

The psychological law of consumption is a generalization about people's consumption habits or, in Keynes's terminology, their *propensity to consume.*

Keynes defined the propensity to consume as "the functional relationship between Y, a given level of income . . . and C the expenditure on consumption out of that level of income" (90). In other words, the propensity to consume is the ratio $\frac{C}{Y}$. This may sound strange, since a propensity is, of course, not a ratio, but an inclination or tendency. Nevertheless, Keynes did define the propensity to consume as a ratio—the ratio $\frac{C}{Y}$.

Distinction must be made between the *average* propensity to consume and the *marginal* propensity to consume. Keynes's definition, quoted in the preceding paragraph, refers to the *average* propensity to consume; it is the average proportion of each income dollar devoted to consumption. If a person has an income of $10,000 and consumes $8,000, he consumes $\frac{4}{5}$ of each income dollar on an average. His average propensity to consume is $\frac{4}{5}$ or 80 per cent.

The *marginal* propensity to consume is the ratio of an *increase* in consumption to an *increase* in income $\dfrac{\triangle C}{\triangle Y}$;[1] or, in other words, the proportion of every *additional* income dollar that is consumed. The psychological law of consumption refers to the *marginal* propensity to consume; it states that men will not *increase* their consumption by as much as the *increase* in their income.

The marginal propensity to consume is generally lower than the average propensity to consume. Most people consume a smaller portion of every *additional* income dollar than they consume of all their income dollars on an average. If the person with a $10,000 income who consumes $8,000 receives an additional $1,000 income, he may decide to increase his consumption expenditures by $500. His *marginal* propensity to consume, in this case, would be ½, or 50 per cent. His *average* propensity to consume, at the $11,000 level of income, would be $\dfrac{8500}{11000} =$ 77 per cent.

In Table 2 (p. 37) and Diagram 2 (p. 38), the *marginal* propensity to consume was assumed to be one-half for all levels of income; consumers were assumed to devote one-half of every additional income dollar to consumption. This assumption was made in order to simplify the illustration. In actual fact, the marginal propensity to consume declines as income increases. An individual may want to consume all of an additional income dollar when his income is $1000 a year, but may want to consume no part of an additional income dollar when his income is $1,000,000 a year.

When analyzing changes in income it is mostly the *marginal* propensity to consume, not the *average* propensity to consume, that needs to be considered. The effect of a change in investment upon income, for instance, will largely depend on the marginal propensity to consume. (See Chapter XI.)

---

1. The symbol $\triangle$ (the Greek letter *delta*) indicates: difference. Thus $\triangle Y$ means the difference, in this case the increment, in income.

PROPENSITY TO CONSUME AND CONSUMPTION FUNCTION

Keynes's definition of the (average) propensity to consume as "the functional relationship between a given level of income and the expenditure on consumption out of that level of income" is identical with his definition of the consumption function. The two terms are used interchangeably by Keynes.

In recent, post-Keynesian economic literature a distinction is usually made between the two terms and a separate meaning is attached to each. The *propensity to consume* refers to an *individual's* schedule of consumption expenditures at various levels of his income. The term *consumption function* is reserved for the entire *community's* income-consumption schedule. Correspondingly, distinction is made between the *marginal propensity to consume,* expressing the relation between an increase in an individual's consumption and an increase in his income; and the *marginal consumption ratio,* which is the name given to the ratio of an increase in the *community's* consumption expenditures to an increase in its income. This terminology will be adhered to throughout the rest of this book.

Keynes did not make a clear distinction between the individual's and the community's income-consumption ratios. He implied that the one is derived from the other, even as the total demand for a particular commodity may be arrived at by adding up all the individuals' demand schedules for that commodity.

It is incorrect, however, to regard the consumption function as merely the sum of the individuals' propensities to consume. The consumption function may change, even though every individual's propensity to consume remains unchanged. This could come about as a result of changes in the distribution of income. If income is taken away from the rich and given to the poor, the rich will not reduce their consumption by as much as the poor will increase theirs. This is in accordance with their respective marginal propensities to consume, for generally people with low incomes have a high marginal propensity to consume, and people with high incomes a low one. The result of the redistribution of income, then, would be to increase the consumption expenditures of the community as a whole, even though aggregate income had remained unchanged and the propensities to consume had remained unchanged.

This leads to the conclusion that the consumption function is affected by the distribution of income, whereas the propensities to consume, i.e., the individuals' consumption schedules, are not affected by it. With given propensities to consume, therefore, there would be as many different consumption functions as there are different ways of distributing the aggregate income. A separate consumption function applies to each possible type of income distribution.

THE CONSUMPTION FUNCTION

In Chapter IV it was explained that the consumption function

1. relates consumption to *real* income,
2. shows that as income increases, consumption increases by a smaller amount,
3. is generally assumed to intersect the income line, which means that at low incomes people may want to consume more than their incomes, while at higher incomes they consume less than their incomes.

Let us now analyze the consumption function further.

Does the consumption function relate consumption to net or gross income?

The consumption function relates the community's aggregate consumption expenditures to income. But what is meant by *income*? *Gross* income, or *net* income?

Gross income (or what Keynes called *income*[2] and what is known in national income accounting as the *Gross National Product*) may be defined as the value of the total output of

2. Keynes defined income as the value of total output minus the "user cost," i.e., the cost which would have had to be incurred to maintain the value of the community's productive equipment even if it had not been used. Though this definition deviates from the usual definition of gross income as the total value of output, we can, for practical purposes, ignore the distinction.

the community. *Net income* (or *Net National Product*) is what is left of gross income after deduction of the value of capital consumed during the period under consideration. Differently stated, *gross* income is the sum of consumption plus *gross* investment; *net* income is the sum of consumption plus *net* investment. (Gross investment consists partly of expenditures for capital equipment to replace equipment used up during the period, partly of net investment, i.e., expenditures for net additions to the community's total stock of capital.)

Net income does not necessarily fluctuate with gross income. The net income, for instance, may change as a result of changes in capital consumption, while gross income—and employment—remain unchanged.

The consumption function is one of the two constituents of aggregate demand; the other constituent being gross investment. The aggregate demand function relates aggregate expenditures to total employment, or, alternatively, to the income produced by the totality of people employed. This income is *gross* income. Accordingly, the consumption function, too, must refer to *gross* income.

On the other hand, it is only the *net* income that is available for consumption; and the community's consumption therefore clearly depends on its *net* income. Most discussions of the consumption function, accordingly, regard this function as showing the relation between consumption and *net* income.

Keynes did not state clearly whether he had *gross* income or *net* income in mind. Perhaps he was confused himself. In one place he said that while employment depends on *gross* income, consumption is "a function of *net* income" (98, italics in original). In another place he stated that "consumption will depend on the level of aggregate income and, therefore, on the level of employment" (28), here clearly meaning *gross* income.[3]

3. In yet another passage Keynes referred to the "heavy drag on the propensity to consume which exists" because of "the deduction [for depreciation] which has to be made from the income of a society, which already possesses a large stock of capital, before we arrive at the net income . . ." (104). Here Keynes apparently again regarded the (com-

[continued on following page]

The question whether the consumption function refers to gross or net income may not be too important. The reason why it is brought up here at all, is that the definition of the consumption function as relating to *net* income has implications for the conventional diagram showing income determination, such as Diagram 4 in this book. Alert students find such diagrams confusing. The difficulty is this: if C in Diagram 4 relates consumption to *net* income, then the Y (Income) axis must measure *net* income. And if this is so, then the investment, which together with consumption determines income, must be *net* investment. Keynes and his interpreters, however, correctly insist that it is *gross* investment which determines (gross) income and employment. Investment in the Keynesian analysis almost invariably means *gross* investment. But if investment is to be understood to mean *gross* investment, then the horizontal axis must measure *gross* income and not *net* income.

The way out of this dilemma is to define the consumption function as relating consumption to *gross* income. This resolves the contradiction, just referred to, in the diagrams showing the determination of income. The definition is not inconsistent with Keynes's own definition, or at least one of his definitions. Besides, the fluctuations in gross and net national income are in most cases fairly parallel, so that it makes little difference which is chosen as the base of reference.

[*continued from preceding page*]

munity's) propensity to consume as relating consumption to gross income, and not to *net* income. If the propensity to consume referred to *net* income, it could not be affected by high depreciation charges. High depreciation charges may be regarded as a "drag" on the net income, but not as a drag on the proportion of net income which people wish to consume.

But possibly Keynes merely expressed himself inaccurately and really meant to say that in a society which already possesses a large stock of capital there is a heavy drag on *consumption* (not on the *propensity to consume*) due to the large depreciation charges that must be deducted from the gross income "before we arrive at the net income which is ordinarily available for consumption" (104). With a given propensity to consume this *net* income, actual consumption would be less when net income is less; and, other things being equal, net income would be less if depreciation charges are higher.

Consumption function affected by tax policies

In the preceding section it was stated that in the Keynesian theory the consumption function must be defined as relating consumption to *gross* income; but that it would be more realistic to define it as relating consumption to *net* income, since only the *net* income is available for consumption. In fact, it is not even the *net* income that is available for consumption, but only the portion of it left after payment of taxes. This residual is called *Disposable Income.* The consumption function should, logically, be defined as the schedule of consumption expenditures corresponding to various levels of *disposable* income.

If defined in this way, as it sometimes is, the consumption function would not be affected by changes in tax rates or tax structure. An increase in taxes would of course reduce the amount of disposable income, but it would not affect the proportion of disposable income which the community consumes.

In the Keynesian analysis, however, where the consumption function expresses the relation between consumption and *gross* income, a change in taxes must be regarded as affecting the consumption function. Any deductions made from the gross income before it becomes available to consumers tends to reduce the amount consumed out of a given gross income, i.e., they lower the consumption function. Taxes constitute such a deduction. Tax policy, consequently, can be an important determinant of the (Keynesian) consumption function.

Consumption function is hypothetical

The consumption function expresses a hypothetical relationship between consumption and income at a particular time. It tells us that *if* income were so and so much today, consumption today would be so and so much; and *if* income were smaller (or larger), consumption would be so and so much. Only one of the many possible amounts of income and of corresponding consumption can be actually realized at one moment. And only the realized income and consumption can be captured and nailed down by the statisticians and reported as an objectively ascertained fact. The function as such can never be statistically ascertained, or empirically verified. It is at best guesswork; often, in theoretical discussions, as in this book, it is based on simple figures assumed with a view to providing an example which will make the basic relationship clear.

While the consumption function is always hypothetical and must forever remain empirically unverifiable, the actual course of consumption over time and in relation to income can, of course, be ascertained statistically. Statistics show that in the short run consumption tends to rise and fall proportionally less than *real* income. This supports the idea that the consumption function is relatively flat, as shown in Diagrams 2, 3 and 4. In the long run, however, consumption has been increasing in about the same proportion as income. This suggests that as real income increases secularly, the consumption function is shifted upward. Keynes, however, dealt with the short run—the time spanning the business cycle—and not with the long run.

Determinants of the consumption function

Changes in the consumption function, i.e., shifts of the consumption function from one position to another, must be ascribed to changes in "objective factors,"[4] of which Keynes listed six:

1. A change in money wages. This possibility should really be ruled out because Keynes himself defined the propensity to consume in terms of *real* income. Nevertheless, changes in money wages, though not changing the size of real income, may change the relative shares of real income going to firms and to *rentiers*. Because these two classes of income recipients may have different propensities to consume, a reshuffling of income between them may affect the consumption function.

2. A change in the difference between gross income and net income. Since Keynes himself doubted the practical importance of this factor, we are justified in neglecting it.

3. Capital gains or losses. Profits made, for instance, on the stock exchange, though they are not income (which results

4. Keynes also listed "subjective" factors. These are given in Chapter X.

only from the current productive activities of the community) may nevertheless induce the community to increase its consumption expenditures.

4. Substantial long-period changes in the rate of interest. Keynes denied that the consumption and saving habits of people are influenced by interest rates, especially in the short run. Substantial long-run changes, however, may affect the consumption function, though it is impossible to say in which direction. A rise in the interest rate may just as easily raise the consumption function as lower it. One person may want to save more in order to harvest the higher interest income. Another person, who wants to accumulate securities to yield him a fixed retirement income, may save less because the higher interest return will enable him to get the desired income from a smaller amount of securities.

5. Changes in fiscal policy, e.g., taxes. Keynes pointed out that by using fiscal policy as a deliberate instrument for the more equal distribution of income, the consumption function could be shifted upward.

6. Changes in expectations of the relation between the present and the future level of income. Keynes minimized the importance of this factor, including it only "for the sake of formal completeness" (95). Professor Hansen, to illustrate how such changes in expectations can cause the consumption function to shift, adduces the example of the Korean War when people rushed to buy goods in the expectation of shortages and of higher prices.[5] Keynes probably did not mean to include the expectation of higher prices here; he referred to *incomes*, not prices. But changes in expectations concerning future prices must surely be counted as an important factor influencing the consumption function. Keynes's omission of this point is remarkable.

5. Hansen, *A Guide to Keynes*, p. 83.

Chapter Ten

Saving

The Keynesian theory is often thought of as showing how intended saving and intended investment together determine income and employment (see p. 54, and Diagram 5, p. 55), in much the same way as pre-Keynesian economists showed how demand and supply determine the exchange value of commodities.

SAVING AS A RESIDUAL

To think of the Keynesian theory as centering around saving and investment is not incorrect. But it misrepresents Keynes's argument in one important respect: according to Keynes it is not *saving*, but *consumption*, the inverse of saving, which, together with investment, determines employment and income. In the Keynesian world people decide how much they will consume, not how much they will save. Of course, having decided how much to consume, people necessarily save the difference between the amount consumed during a given period and the income received during that same period. Saving is a "mere residual"—it is the part of income which is not consumed.

CLASSICAL AND KEYNESIAN VIEWS OF SAVING

This conception differs from the classical view. The classical economists regarded saving as a deliberate act; they thought of people deciding how much they will save and then of consuming what is left over of their incomes. Thus the classical economists treated consumption rather than saving as the residual.

There is a second difference between the classical and the Keynesian concepts of saving. The classical economists thought of saving as "postponing consumption"; Keynes said saving is simply "not consuming"—whether now or later. Of course a person may consume tomorrow or next year what he has saved today. But the future consumption is not implied, nor usually intended, in the present act of saving.

The real significance of these different ways of looking at saving lies in the support which they lend to different ideologies rather than in any light they may shed on the actual behavior of people as consumers and savers. By defining saving as "postponed consumption" the classical economists evoked the idea of abnegation or sacrifice on the part of the saver. This abnegation they regarded as socially beneficial because it leads to the accumulation of capital. Saving is good, consuming is bad. Therefore the saver receives a justified reward in the form of interest. This argument extolls the role of the *rentier*—the man who saves and clips coupons—and shows him as deserving a reward for virtue.

In the Keynesian system the *rentier* is useless, in fact harmful. He saves not because he is virtuous, but because a psychological "law" compels him to consume less than his income. There is no abnegation or sacrifice in saving. No reward is called for. Far from being socially beneficial, saving is merely "a drag on consumption" and must be discouraged. Consumption must be encouraged. The consumer is exalted; the *rentier*, the "useless investor," is condemned to "euthanasia"—a pleasant, or at least a non-violent, death.

MOTIVES FOR SAVING

Since Keynes regarded saving as a passive, negative corollary of consumption, he gave his attention to consumption, and not to saving; and accordingly he inquired into the reasons why people *consume*, rather than into the reasons why they *save*. He listed a number of "subjective" and "objective" factors determining the propensity to *consume*. (The "objective" factors were listed in the preceding chapter; they explain why the consumption function may shift.) The "subjective" factors, however, are clearly motives for *saving*, and not motives for *consuming*. They may be regarded as the determinants of the *propensity to save*, i.e., the propensity to *not* consume. These subjective factors determining the propensity to save are:

1. To build up a reserve against unforeseen contingencies.
2. To provide for education, old age, and so on.
3. To get an income from accumulated wealth.
4. To enjoy gradually increasing expenditures.
5. To enjoy a sense of independence and power.
6. To secure a *masse de manoeuvre* to carry out speculative or business projects.
7. To bequeath a fortune.
8. To satisfy pure miserliness.

"These eight motives might be called the motives of Precaution, Foresight, Calculation, Improvement, Independence, Enterprise, Pride and Avarice; and," Keynes added in an attempt to center attention on *consumption*, "we could also draw up a corresponding list of motives to consumption such as Enjoyment, Shortsightedness, Generosity, Miscalculation, Ostentation and Extravagance" (108).

Keynes added four motives for saving by corporations and governments:

1. The motive of enterprise. (Firms want to accumulate the means for new ventures.)
2. The motive of liquidity.
3. The motive of improvement, i.e., to increase income gradually.
4. The motive of financial prudence.

Saving and consumption governed by custom

These twelve motives, then, account for the propensity to save. A change in the intensity of one or several or all of these motives may change the propensity to save. But Keynes assumed that these "subjective" factors, reflecting the prevailing habits and customs of the community, would not change significantly in the short run. Consequently the propensity to save—and the propensity to consume—are not likely to change much in the short run.

Since Keynes made much of the element of custom and habit in determining *saving*, it is strange that he did not make more of this factor as a determinant of consumption. He did point out that consumption is largely dictated by custom; that a person's habitual standard of living prescribes his consumption expenditures. But, strangely, he did not include this in the "subjective factors" determining the propensity to *consume*.

THE PROPENSITY TO SAVE AND
THE SAVING FUNCTION

As we speak of the average and marginal propensity to *consume*, so we also speak of the average and marginal propensity to *save*. The average propensity to save is the ratio of saving to income; the marginal propensity to save is the ratio of an increase in saving to an increase in income. We can also define the average propensity to save as the inverse of the average propensity to consume, i.e., 1 minus average propensity to consume. Thus, if the average propensity to consume is $\frac{4}{5}$, the average propensity to save is $\frac{1}{5}$. Similarly, the marginal propensity to save is 1 minus marginal propensity to consume.

Corresponding to the concept of the consumption function, there is also a *saving function*, which may be defined as the functional relationship between given amounts of aggregate income and the amounts which the community intends to save out of these given amounts of income. The saving function is illustrated by Table 4 (page 54) and by the S line in Diagram 5 (page 55). The saving function is the inverse of the consumption function; for every level of aggregate income, saving is income minus consumption.

THE SAVING FUNCTION AND THE AMOUNT SAVED

As previously in connection with the consumption function, so here again attention must be called to the difference between changes in the propensity to save or in the saving function on the one hand, and changes in the actual amount saved on the other hand. The saving function may rise, i.e., the community may wish to save a greater part of its income, yet actual saving may remain unchanged, or even decline, because aggregate income declines; and vice versa. Again, the saving *function* may remain unchanged, while *actual* saving fluctuates in response to changes in aggregate income.

The actual amount of saving, it will be remembered, is determined solely by the amount of *investment* and must always be exactly equal to the amount of investment. Given the saving function, the community is willing to save this amount only out of one particular level of aggregate income. Aggregate income will therefore gravitate toward that level.

Chapter Eleven

The Multiplier

The concept of the multiplier was briefly introduced in Chapter VI. In the present chapter this concept is more fully analyzed.

Keynes said that changes in investment must be associated with corresponding changes in saving, and these changes in saving can occur only as a result of changes in real income—assuming, of course, that the community's parsimony, i.e., the saving function, remains unchanged. Thus, to illustrate the point with a numerical example, let us assume that a hypothetical community wants to save 10 per cent of its income, regardless of the level of income. If investment in this community runs at the rate of 25 billion dollars a year, saving must also be at the rate of 25 billion dollars a year, and since saving represents 10 per cent of the community's income, this income must be at the rate of 250 billion dollars. Now suppose that investment increases to 30 billion dollars. Saving of course must also increase to 30 billion dollars. But people will save 30 billion dollars only if their income is 300 billion dollars. Income consequently must rise to 300 billion dollars in our imaginary community, if investment rises to 30 billion. A 5 billion increase in investment is associated with a 50 billion increase in income. Any increase (or decrease) in investment brings with it a tenfold increase (or decrease) in income. The *multiplier,* expressed by the symbol k, in this case is 10. The multiplier may be defined as the number by which increases (or decreases) in investment must be multiplied in order to give us the increase (or decrease) in aggregate income associated with the change in investment.

THE MARGINAL CONSUMPTION
RATIO AND THE MULTIPLIER

It is easy to see that, given the saving function (i.e., the schedule of the community's saving at various levels of income), the increased saving required by increased investment can come only out of an income enlarged by a multiple of the increment in investment. But just how does this enlargement of income come about? It comes about partly as a result of a *primary* or *direct* effect of investment on income, and partly as a result of a *secondary* or *indirect* effect of investment on in- come. The primary effect is that any additional investment automatically also constitutes additional income, since income, it will be remembered, is always equal to the sum of consumption and investment ($Y = C + I$). The secondary effect is that people increase their consumption expenditures when investment, and consequently also income, increases. But additional expenditures of consumers also constitute additional income for those who sell the consumer goods and this additional income leads to further increases in consumer expenditures and to further increases in income in a continuing process.

How far will this process go? By how much, in the final analysis, will the community's consumption and income increase as a result of an increase in investment? This depends on the *marginal consumption ratio,* that is, on the proportion of each additional dollar of income which the community devotes to additional consumption. It should be noted that what matters in this connection is the *marginal* consumption ratio, not the *average* consumption ratio (i.e., consumption function).

Multiplier is reciprocal of marginal saving ratio

If the marginal consumption ratio were $\frac{2}{3}$, and the marginal saving ratio therefore $\frac{1}{3}$, the multiplier would be 3. If the marginal consumption ratio were $\frac{9}{10}$ and the community saved only 10 per cent of any additional income, the multiplier would be 10. The greater the additional consumption generated by an addition to income, the greater must be the multiplier effect of an additional investment. Or, the smaller the additional saving called forth by additional income, the greater must be the multiplier. The multiplier is the reciprocal of the marginal saving ratio (MSR), i.e., $\dfrac{1}{\text{MSR}}$. Since the MSR is the inverse of the marginal consumption ratio (MCR), the multiplier can also be expressed as $\dfrac{1}{1-\text{MCR}}$.

ILLUSTRATION OF THE MULTIPLIER

Again an example may serve best to clarify the multiplier effect of investment. Let us assume that the directors of a firm decide to enlarge their plant at a cost of $1000 and that this $1000 investment constitutes a net addition to the aggregate investment of the community. How the investment is financed is of no importance. The firm may have accumulated the needed media of payment out of previous sales receipts, or it may have received them from stockholders, or borrowed them. To simplify the example it may be assumed that the investment expenditure is made at one moment rather than over a period of time. The $1000 is paid out today to the several people—architect, suppliers, workmen—who have contributed to the enlargement of the plant. A further assumption must be made with respect to the community's marginal consumption ratio. Let us say it is ⅔, meaning that for every dollar of additional income, people increase their consumption expenditures by 67 cents. The expansion of income associated with the additional investment is shown in Table 5.

The additional investment gives rise directly to an equal amount of additional income; the $1000 paid out by the firm constitutes at the same time an investment expenditure by the firm and income for the architect, the suppliers, the workmen, and other recipients of the $1000 paid out by the firm. On the strength of their increased income these people then devote $677, or ⅔ of $1000, to additional consumption, and they save an additional $333, or ⅓ of $1000. The $677 spent on con-

TABLE 5
Multiplier Effect—Expansion

Additional investment	Additional income $\triangle Y$	Additional consumption $\triangle C = \frac{2}{3}\triangle Y$	Additional saving $\triangle S = \frac{1}{3}\triangle Y$
$1000 ⟶	$1000	$	$
	667	667	333
	445	445	222
	296	296	148
	'	198	98
	,	,	,
$1000	$3000	$2000	$1000

sumption immediately becomes additional income for those who supplied the additional goods and services consumed. The recipients of this additional income in their turn increase their consumption expenditures by $\frac{2}{3}$, and their saving by $\frac{1}{3}$ of the additional income, i.e., by $445 and $222, respectively. The $445 spent on consumption in this third round again becomes income, again leading to further increases in consumption and saving. The sums of these increases in income, consumption, and saving are shown in the bottom line of the table.[1] The end result of cumulative increases in income is $3000, while the successive increases in consumption total up to $2000 and saving to $1000 —a sum exactly equal to the investment which set off the whole cycle of increases.

1. The formula for finding the sum to infinity of a diminishing series a, ar, ar², . . . is $\dfrac{a}{1-r}$. Thus $1 + \frac{2}{3} + (\frac{2}{3})^2 \ldots = \dfrac{1}{1-\frac{2}{3}} = \dfrac{1}{\frac{1}{3}} = 3$.

THE MULTIPLIER IN REVERSE

The multiplier applies not only to increases in investment leading to multiple increases in income, but operates also in reverse: reductions in investment, or *dis*investment, cause income to contract by a multiple of the disinvestment. A decline in investment has the primary effect of reducing income by an equal amount. The people suffering the income reduction respond in part by saving less than they had intended to save and in part by reducing their consumption. This in turn reduces the income of others who again react partly by curtailing their consumption, and so on. The end result of the process is that income will have shrunk by a multiple (depending on the marginal consumption ratio) of the reduction in investment, as shown in Table 6.

TABLE 6

Multiplier Effect—Contraction

Investment	Reduction in income $\triangle Y$	Reduction in consumption $\triangle C = \frac{2}{3}\triangle Y$	Reduction in saving $\triangle S = \frac{1}{3}\triangle Y$
− $ 1000	− $ 1000	$	$
	− 667	− 667	− 333
	− 445	− 445	− 222
	− 296	− 296	− 148
	,	,	,
	,	,	,
− $ 1000	− $ 3000	$ − 2000	$ − 1000

MULTIPLIER EFFECT OF CHANGE IN THE RATE OF INVESTMENT

In Table 5, the investment of $1000 was assumed to be a single, non-recurring expenditure and the multiplier effect of this single investment expenditure was traced through. It would be more realistic, however, to assume a change in the *rate of investment*, which means that day after day more (or less) is being invested than was invested day after day before the change occurred. For example, let us say that last year a community, such as the United States, invested $30 billion—spread evenly over the entire year, to make it simpler; but this year it invests, say, $35 billion a year. The *rate* of investment is $5 billion higher this year than it was last year.

What would be the multiplier effect of an increase in the *rate* of investment?

When the *rate* of investment increases, each successive day's increased investment would set off its own multiplier effect which must be added to the multiplier effect of the previous day's increased investment. Thus, if additional investment were $1000 day after day, and again assuming a marginal consumption ratio of ⅔, the multiplier effect would be as shown in Table 7.

The effect of the first day's investment of $1000 is to increase income by $1000. On the second day investment will again add $1000 to income, but there will also be additional consumption of $667, since we assumed that people consume ⅔ of the additional income of $1000 they received yesterday.[2] The total increase in income on the second day (or whatever period elapses before people increase their consumption) will, therefore, be $1667. On the third day consumers will consume ⅔ of this amount, or $1112, while investment adds another $1000, making the total increase in income for the third day $2112. Each successive day, as additional investment expenditures continue to add $1000 to income, additional consumption will increase until the daily additional consumption reaches $2000, and the daily additional income reaches $3000. At this point the multiplier will have increased the *rate* of income by three times the additional *rate* of investment; unless and until the rate of investment changes again, additional investment,

2. Of course, people may not increase their consumption on the day after they received the additional income, but perhaps a month or two months later. But however delayed, the effects will be essentially as described in the text and as shown in Table 7.

TABLE 7

Multiplier Effect of Increase in Rate of Investment

	Additional investment		Additional consumption		Additional income
First day	$ 1000 ————————	$	———————————→		$ 1000
Second day	1000	+	667 ←	=	1667
Third day	1000	+	1112 ←	=	2112
Fourth day	1000	+	1408 ←	=	2408
	,		, ←		,
	,		,		,
	1000	+	2000 ←	=	3000
	1000	+	2000 ←	=	3000
	1000	+	2000 ←	=	3000

consumption, and income will continue unchanged day after day. The principle is the same as in the case of the non-recurring investment, illustrated in Table 5.

MULTIPLIER EFFECT REQUIRES TIME TO WORK ITSELF OUT

The above illustration of the multiplier effect suggests that it takes time for this effect to work itself out. In fact, it takes infinitely long for the multiplier effect set in motion by an investment expenditure to work itself out completely, until the last ripple caused by the injection of the additional investment has died down and the economy has reached a new equilibrium. For practical purposes, however, only the first few rounds of increases in Y and C need to be considered, since in subsequent ones the amounts involved become negligibly small. If it takes consumers two months on an average to respond to increases in their income by enlarging their consumption expenditures—in other words, if each successive round of increases in income and consumption represents a time span of two months—then it would take about a year for the main effect of the multiplier to have spent itself.

THE LOGICAL THEORY OF THE MULTIPLIER

Keynes, however, did not treat the multiplier effect as something that requires time to work itself out. Instead, he assumed that whenever changes in investment occur, consumption changes simultaneously by the amount necessary to keep the economy in equilibrium. Thus if investment (I) increased by $1000, and the marginal consumption ratio were $\frac{2}{3}$, as assumed in the illustration on pages 85-86, Chapter XI, production and consumption of consumers' goods (C) would simultaneously increase by $2000, and income (Y, which equals C + I), would simultaneously increase by $3000. In this way the equilibrium relation between I and C would not be disturbed by any changes in investment and restored only after a lapse of time, but would be maintained continuously, as a "moving equilibrium." Keynes called his multiplier theory the "logical theory of the multiplier," in contrast to the "time-lag theory of the multiplier."

That Keynes chose the "logical" theory of the multiplier in preference to the "time-lag" theory stems from his desire to cut through the complications of tracing out the minutiae of the process by which the economy adjusts itself to changes in any of the significant variables. To achieve this aim he centered his attention on the new situation resulting from such changes after all the interim adjustments have been made. In other words, Keynes assumed that the economy immediately jumps to a new "equilibrium" position in response to any change in any variable; or, rather, as already mentioned above, that the economy never gets out of equilibrium but remains in a state of "moving equilibrium."

This method of analysis is often referred to as the "static" method, in contrast to the "dynamic" method which traces the paths by which the economy returns to a state of equilibrium when equilibrium has been disturbed. Although Keynes's analysis is static rather than dynamic in the sense just stated, it is nevertheless dynamic in the sense that it is concerned with economic motion. It must be remembered that Keynes was primarily interested in discovering and explaining why employment, output, and income are continuously fluctuating.

SIGNIFICANCE OF MULTIPLIER THEORY

The difference between the two interpretations of the multiplier—the "logical" and the "time-lag" interpretations—has no practical significance. The important truth contained in the multiplier principle is revealed by both interpretations: that, other things remaining equal, increases (or decreases) in investment must always be associated with greater increases (or decreases) in income, and that the magnitude of the change in income resulting from a given change in investment depends on the magnitude of the multiplier. This important relationship was not understood by pre-Keynesian economists, who maintained that changes in investment are not accompanied by any change at all in income, because any increase in investment must be offset by a corresponding decrease in consumption, and any decrease in investment must be offset by a corresponding increase in consumption. As Keynes showed, this doctrine of the inverse relationship between I and C holds true only for the case of full employment, in which output and (real) income as a whole, in the short run, cannot change. In the usual case of less than full employment, however, C and I fluctuate in the same direction, and not inversely, and consequently output and income as a whole, Y, fluctuate by a multiple of changes in investment.

The importance of the multiplier principle lies chiefly in its implications for economic policy; it provides the justification for public works (and for government expenditures generally) as a means of lifting a depressed economy to higher levels of income and employment. Keynes credited R. F. Kahn with having first formulated the multiplier principle in an article on "The Relation of Home Investment to Unemployment" in *The Economic Journal,* June, 1931.

EMPLOYMENT MULTIPLIER AND INVESTMENT MULTIPLIER

The multiplier as here explained is called the *investment multiplier* (k) to distinguish it from the *employment multiplier* (k'). The investment multiplier relates an increase (or decrease) in *investment expenditures* to the resulting increase (or decrease) in *income.* The employment multiplier relates an increase (decrease) in *employment in the investment* (or *capital goods*) *industries* to the resulting increase (decrease) in *total employment.*

These two multiplier concepts are not quite the same. An additional investment expenditure of $50,000, for instance, may require the employment of ten additional men in the investment goods industries. The corresponding increase of $100,000 in consumption (again assuming a marginal consumption ratio of ⅔) on the other hand, may require the employment of only eighteen additional men in the consumer goods industries. There is no reason to suppose that the amount of labor required to produce an additional dollar's worth of goods is the same in every industry.

For practical purposes, however, we can assume, as Keynes himself did that k = k', so that if an increase in investment leads to a 10 per cent rise in income, it will also lead to a 10 per cent rise in employment. This is merely another aspect of the assumption that income and employment fluctuate together and in the same degree.

LEAKAGES

If people did not want to save, the effect of an additional investment of $1000 would be to create a further additional income of $1000 at every subsequent income—consumption round in which additional income is received and consumed, on and on, without end. The multiplier would be infinitely large. But k is in fact *not* infinitely large. A $1000 investment does *not* set off an endless expansion of income. Some of the income-generating power of the additional investment "leaks" away.

This "leakage" is explained primarily by the fact that in most situations people do want to save a part of their additional income. Saving on the part of consumers is the principal cause of leakage. But there are other causes of leakage. One of them is that also corporations "save,"—by withholding corporate profits from stockholders. Further leakages are due to taxes which take away some of the additional income in each successive round. Finally, some of the income-creating power of an additional investment leaks away to foreign countries. Up to this point in the present chapter it was tacitly assumed that the economy is "closed"—that it is entirely self-sufficient and has no external relations. In actual fact, countries do of course have external economic relations. In some cases as much as 50 per cent or more of all goods consumed come from foreign countries, and a similar proportion of domestically produced goods is exported to foreign countries. In a country which imports much of what it consumes, the "leakage" due to additional imports resulting from an increase in income will be considerable. To the extent to which additional income is used to buy foreign goods, it has no further effect on domestic consumption and income (except in so far as purchases from foreign countries also tend to increase sales to foreign countries). Instead, the multiplier effect is transferred to the foreign countries from which the goods were bought.

MULTIPLIER EFFECTS OF
ADDITIONAL CONSUMPTION

Keynes ascribed the multiplier effects only to changes in investment. In fact, however, any additional expenditure—whether for consumption or investment—tends to set off a multiple expansion of income, and any reduction in expenditures—whether for consumption or investment—sets off a multiple contraction of income.

Keynes neglected the multiplier effects of consumption because he assumed that the consumption function is stable in the short run—and his analysis was a short run analysis. With a given C function, a change in Y can arise only from a change in I; the (C + I) function can rise only if I increases (see Diagram 4). But if the C function is *not* assumed to be unchanging, the rise in the (C + I) function could be due to a shift in the C function as well as to a shift in the I function. A change in the proportion of their incomes which people decide to consume has the same multiple effect on incomes as has a change in investment expenditures.

THE SUPER-MULTIPLIER

As mentioned earlier (Chapter V, page 49), Keynes also failed to consider the so-called acceleration effect, which is the effect of a change in consumption on investment. He assumed that investment is independent of the level of income; that fluctuations in investment are the prime determinants of changes in income, but that they are not themselves determined by fluctuations in income. This is why the investment function in Diagrams 4 and 5 was shown as a horizontal line. Actually, however, investment does fluctuate in response to changes in consumption and consequently also in response to changes in income. Although some investment expenditures are *autonomous* (i.e., independent of the level of consumption and income), others are *induced* (i.e., dependent on the level of consumption and income). The investment function should, therefore, be shown as a line slanting upward to the right.

The acceleration effect is generally understood to mean, as pointed out above, the change in investment called forth by a change in *consumption*. Investment, however, may be induced not only by changes in consumption, but by any changes in income, whether these are due to changes in consumption or investment. Thus, for instance, a large-scale road building program, which must certainly be classed as an investment, is likely to induce manufacturers of road building equipment to invest in order to expand their plants. The acceleration effect may, therefore, be taken to mean that any primary increase (or decrease) in income, whether attributable to investment or consumption or both, induces a secondary increase (or decrease) in investment. This redefinition of the acceleration effect parallels our earlier redefinition of the multiplier effect as referring to the secondary increase in income called forth by a primary increase in income, whether attributable to investment or consumption or both. When the acceleration effect is combined with the multiplier effect, when account is taken of the mutual effects which changes in consumption and investment have upon each other, we get a "super-multiplier." This super-multiplier must always be greater than the simple multiplier; it indicates that fluctuations in employment, output, and income set off by any changes in investment or consumption are even greater than would appear if only the simple multiplier and acceleration effects were at work.[3]

3. Cf. Kurihara, *Introduction to Keynesian Dynamics* pp. 88-89.

Chapter Twelve

Saving Equals Investment

Two propositions set forth by Keynes regarding the relation between saving and investment continue to give trouble to the student and to be resisted with incredulity. These propositions are:

1. Saving is equal to investment
2. Saving is determined by investment (i.e., saving results from investment).

In the present chapter the first of these propositions will be explored. The second proposition will be the subject of the next chapter.

PROOF OF EQUALITY OF S AND I

Keynes asserted that S is always equal to I. That this must be so is proved by the following syllogism:

Income is always the sum of consumption expenditures and investment expenditures. $Y = C + I$, or: $I = Y - C$.

Income is always either consumed or saved. $Y = C + S$, or: $S = Y - C$.

Therefore $I = S$.

This proposition may appear simple and obvious, yet seems difficult to accept. The difficulty stems from the observation that an individual may save more or less than the amounts he invests; and that, moreover, the people who save are not the same as those who invest. Why should savers always spontaneously decide to save amounts equal to the amounts which others decide to invest? Did Keynes perhaps mean that S and

I are *approximately* equal? Or that there is a *tendency* for S to equal I, but that S would actually not be equal to I except in "equilibrium"?

The answer to these questions is that S equals I, to the penny, under all circumstances and at all times.

EQUALITY OF S AND I DEPENDS ON DEFINITIONS

It should be understood at the outset that the statement S = I necessarily depends on the definitions of S and I. The two magnitudes are equal on Keynes's definitions, but not necessarily on other definitions. Those who doubt the proposition that S = I often have such other definitions in mind, though perhaps they are not aware of it.

Keynes's Earlier Definition of Saving

One source of confusion is that, before writing the *General Theory*, Keynes himself had defined saving in such a way that S and I could be unequal. His argument in the *Treatise on Money* (1930), had revolved around this *in*equality of S and I. (See Chapter XXI, below.) In that work Keynes had defined S as including only saving out of factor incomes and normal profit, but excluding saving out of abnormal, or windfall, profits. Saving so defined does not equal investment, except in equilibrium, when there are no abnormal profits or losses. In the *General Theory* S is defined as including saving out of abnormal profit, or, in other words, saving is defined as saving out of aggregate income. On that definition S always equals I.

Saving in period analysis

A second source of confusion is that people often think of S and I as pertaining to different income periods. The amount saved out of yesterday's income is not related to the amount invested today. If S and I are defined in this sense, the equality of S and I does not hold. In the so-called "period analysis," "today's" income (Y) is not consumed or saved until "tomorrow." "Today's" consumption is made out of "yesterday's" Y. The part

of "yesterday's" Y which is not consumed "today" is "today's"
S. This S is independent of "today's" I and may be larger or
smaller than "today's" I.

Keynes did not use period analysis, but defined Y, C, I, and
S as all pertaining to the same period. Only if viewed in this
way is it true that S = I.

Intended S and I and actual S and I

A third source of confusion is the failure to distinguish between the amount the community *intends* to save and invest,
and the amount *actually* saved and invested. The amount the
community *intends* to save may be different from the amount
it *intends* to invest. It is only the *actual* amount saved which
must, in all cases, be equal to the *actual* amount invested.

Equilibrium and the equality of S and I

The confusion between *intended* and *actual* S and I is unfortunately abetted by the custom of using the same symbols,
S and I, in both cases.

Diagram 5, for instance, shows the S and I lines intersecting.
If S were always equal to I, the two lines should be identical.
If they are shown as intersecting, then S = I only at the point
of intersection, which marks the "equilibrium" position of the
economy. Accordingly S and I would seem to be equal only in
"equilibrium."

The reader will recall that this contradiction was explained
and resolved in Chapter VIII. There it was explained that the
C function must be understood to show the amounts which the
community *intends* to spend on consumption out of various
levels of income. The S function correspondingly shows what
the community *intends* to save out of various levels of income.
And the I function shows *intended* investment and not actual
investment.

The point of intersection between the *intended* S and *intended*
I lines marks the equilibrium position of the economy. *Actual*
S is always equal to *actual* I, regardless of whether the economy
is in equilibrium or not.

EQUALITY OF S AND I AND
THE MULTIPLIER TIME-LAG

The analysis of the multiplier in Chapter XI also seems to cast doubt on the proposition that S = I. Tables 5, 6, and 7 suggest that S will equal I only at the end of the (infinitely long) period which must elapse before the multiplier has worked itself out; and that, therefore, S is not equal to I until that time; that, in other words, S is never really exactly equal to I but merely *tends* to equal I. This, however, would be an incorrect conclusion. The equality of S and I remains unimpaired throughout the process of adjustment of consumption and income to the increased investment.

The first recipients of the $1000 expended in enlarging the plant (see Table 5), may want to save only $333 of this additional income, and consume $667 of it, as we have assumed. But until they get around to spending the $667 on consumption, they must save this amount willy-nilly. In other words, they save the entire additional income until they consume a part of it. When the first recipients of the investment expenditure have spent the $667, the people in the next round, who find themselves with additional income of $667 must save it all until they, in turn, consume a part of their additional income. And so, in every subsequent income-consumption round, the additional income is saved until it is partly consumed and becomes income for others who must save it until they partly consume it.

The total additional amount saved, therefore, is $1000 from the moment the investment expenditure was made; but some portion—a steadily decreasing portion—of this amount is *unintentionally* saved. Only when the multiplier has run its full course has the entire $1000 been saved *intentionally*. At that point actual saving will of course be equal to investment, which it must always be, and, in addition, intended saving will be equal to the amount invested. This is the same as to say that only when the multiplier has run its full course will income have regained its equilibrium level, namely that level at which the community intends to save an amount exactly equal to the amount of intended investment.

The "fallacy of composition"

A chief reason why many people find it difficult to accept the proposition that S = I is that they think that what is true for any individual must also be true for the community as a whole. The false assumption that this must be so is known as the "fallacy of composition."

It is true that every individual member of a community can save more or less than he invests. But it is not true that an entire community can do so. Even an individual cannot save more or less than he invests, if he lives in isolation. Robinson Crusoe necessarily had to save exactly as much as he invested. When he built a canoe or a shelter—a capital expenditure of his effort— he saved that part of his output (or of his income, which is the same thing) because he did not consume it. When he saved part of the food he had gathered, he also invested because he added the unconsumed portion of food to his stock of goods. But the moment Robinson was joined by Friday it would have been possible for either of them to save more than he invested, or vice versa. Robinson, for instance, could have invested by devoting a day's labor to building a canoe and yet could have consumed the entire value of his day's labor, thus saving nothing. He could have done so by getting the consumables from Friday. Friday could have devoted his efforts on the same day to producing food, but he might have consumed none of it, thus saving his entire day's income and letting Robinson consume it. Nevertheless, for the entire community—consisting of Robinson and Friday—saving would have remained equal to investment. If Friday was willing to save only half the value of the canoe, Robinson necessarily had to save the other half. Together, they had to save an amount equal to the value of the canoe.

In the real world it is the same, though the relations between S and I are more complex and hence not so easily seen. We may think of the community as consisting of two groups: the Fridays, the individuals who save; and the Robinsons, the firms which invest and also save. In so far as the Fridays do not save amounts equal to the additions made by firms to the value of capital, the firms save. Together, firms and individuals,

Robinsons and Fridays, are bound to save amounts exactly equal to the amounts invested.

The proposition that the aggregate amounts saved always equal the aggregate amounts invested, though for every individual or firm the amounts saved are not equal to the amounts invested, has several analogies which are more readily accepted and which may help to drive home the logic of S = I:

1. The aggregate of exports from all countries must equal aggregate imports by all countries. Everything that is exported from one country must be imported by some other country. Yet any one country may export more or less than it imports.

2. Aggregate sales must equal aggregate purchases. Everything that is sold must necessarily be purchased by someone. Yet any individual may buy more or less than he sells.

3. The aggregate of all debts must equal the aggregate of all claims. Every debt incurred by a debtor must necessarily at the same time represent a claim acquired by a creditor. Yet any individual may acquire claims in excess of the debts he incurs, or vice versa.

In the same way and for the same reasons aggregate saving must equal aggregate investment. Every dollar's worth of additions to capital must represent income not consumed by some saver. Yet any individual may save more or less than he invests.

Chapter Thirteen

Saving is Determined by Investment

In the preceding chapter it was shown that the amounts actually saved must always equal the amounts actually invested. The second troublesome proposition set forth by Keynes regarding the relation between S and I is that S is determined by I. This is the subject of the present chapter.

I DETERMINES S

Keynes said that the aggregate amounts saved in a community during any period depend solely on the amounts that have been invested during that same period. If no investment takes place, nothing is saved, regardless of how great the community's desire to save may be. If much is invested, correspondingly much is saved, regardless of how weak the community's desire to save may be. That this must be so can be seen most clearly when attention is centered on *real* processes. A community's real saving consists of not consuming all of its real income. Its real income is the total of goods produced during a given period. If some of these goods were not consumed, they must have been added to the community's stock of goods, either in the form of additional capital equipment or in the form of additional inventories. But such additions to capital equipment and inventories are precisely what is meant by real *investment*. They are the *real* additions to capital, corresponding to the investment *expenditures* incurred for the purpose of making these additions. (See Chapter V.) Without investment on the part of firms which increase their capital equipment or their inventories there would be no increase in capital—and consequently there would be no saving either. S, therefore, is the reflection of I; the amounts saved depend upon, are determined by, how much has been invested.

COMMON-SENSE VIEW THAT I DEPENDS ON S

Incontrovertible though it may seem when looked at in real terms, this interpretation of the relation between S and I seems to be contradicted by the common-sense proposition that people must save before their savings can be invested. Regardless of how much firms may desire to expand their capital equipment, the community as a whole will be unable to invest more than what people have been willing to save. And there is no reason to suppose that their willingness to save is affected by the firms' desire to invest.

In the light of these considerations, it would seem that it is I which is determined by S, and not the other way around. This was indeed regarded as self-evident by pre-Keynesian economists. The same view continues to be widely held among present-day economists, especially by business economists. We are continually being admonished to save more in order to make possible the larger volume of investment needed for greater economic progress.

CONFLICTING INTERPRETATIONS
PARTLY DUE TO DEFINITIONS

To some extent the conflict between the two opposing interpretations of the relation between S and I arises from definitions and assumptions, even as the equality of S and I was shown to depend on definitions. Here again, attention must be called to the distinction between *intended* saving and *actual* saving. It is the amount *actually* saved, not the S function, which is determined by I. The S function is independent of I. But with a given S function, the amount actually saved—and the corresponding level of income—is determined by I.

Also as in the case of the equality of S and I, the definitions used in "period analysis" would vitiate the proposition that I determines S. In period analysis I and S are defined as pertaining to different income periods and are consequently independent of each other. In Keynes's theory I and S belong to the same period and it is only when defined in this sense that I determines S.

The proposition that I determines S also hinges on whether I is defined as intended I or unintended I. If it were conceded that some I may be unintended, then it would be correct to say that I is determined by S. Thus, for instance, the community may want to save more (and consume correspondingly less) at a given level of income than the amounts which firms want to invest. As a result, goods remain unsold on the sellers' shelves. This unintended investment in enlarged inventories is the result of the community's saving. It will be remembered, however, that Keynes disregarded unintended I and assumed that all additions to capital result from *intended* I.[1] On this assumption the amount saved must be determined by the amount invested.

DOES I DETERMINE S IN FULL EMPLOYMENT?

Much of the Keynesian theory applies only to the case of less-than-full employment, while in the case of full employment the pre-Keynesian, "classical" theory continues to hold. Does the proposition that S is determined by I also cease to hold in the case of full employment?

On Keynes's definition the amount saved is always determined by the volume of investment, even in full employment. Nevertheless, there is an important difference between the S : I relationship in less-than-full employment and in full employment. As long as there is less-than-full employment, an increase in I calls forth additional *real* saving by raising *real* income (Y) to higher levels. Y rises because consumption (C) rises concomitantly with I in accordance with the multiplier. But once

1. Keynes had to assume this because he assumed that the economy is always in equilibrium and adjusts itself instantaneously to any changes in the C function or in I. In equilibrium there cannot be any unintended I, because by definition, equilibrium is a situation in which intended I equals intended S. Unintended changes in inventories can occur only as a result of the disruption of equilibrium and in the process of transition to a new position of equilibrium.

full employment is reached, this mechanism which causes an increase in I to call forth additional S by raising real C and real Y can no longer be operative. If I is increased under conditions of full employment, C (i.e., *real* C, or the output of consumption goods), so far from being *in*creased, must be correspondingly *decreased*, since, by definition, real Y cannot be expanded further. There is no reason, however, to assume that the community would *want* to curtail its consumption and to save more, or, in other words, that the saving function would rise. Pressure of demand for consumption goods would, therefore, induce firms to expand output of consumption goods and correspondingly to reduce the output of investment goods. Presumably this increase in the output of consumption goods would continue until the relative quantities of output of consumption goods and investment goods correspond to the proportions in which the community wants to allocate its income to consumption and to saving, respectively.[2]

It would seem, therefore, that investment (I)—in full employment—depends on the amounts which the community is willing to save out of full employment Y; and that an increase in I—in full employment—could take place only if the saving function were raised, in other words, if the community were willing to save more. Nevertheless, it remains true that even in full employment the actual amount saved by the community as a whole must be determined by I. If I exceeds the amount which the community intends to save, the community will nevertheless be forced to save, willy-nilly, because of its inability to get the desired quantities of consumption goods.

DOES INVESTMENT DEPEND ON THE AVAILABILITY OF "INVESTMENT FUNDS"?

In the preceding sections some qualifications and exceptions to the proposition that I determines S have been noted. But those who deny the proposition and who assert that investment can-

---

2. This conclusion, however, rests on the assumptions that the market and price mechanisms actually indicate consumer choices and that firms are guided by these indications. It is questionable to what extent these assumptions correspond to reality.

not take place unless there has been previous saving, do not ordinarily rest their case on any of the above mentioned arguments. Their principal line of reasoning is that before an investor can make an investment expenditure, he must have the "funds" with which to make it. He must either have previously saved these "funds" himself, or he must get them from others who have previously saved them and who are willing to make their savings available to firms needing "investment funds."

This reasoning contains a number of fallacies concerning the nature of "funds" and their connection with saving and investment. The remaining part of this chapter is devoted to an attempt to unravel these fallacies.

What are "funds"?

The term "funds" has many meanings. In economics it means "pecuniary resources," i.e., "sums of money." Thus, when we say that we are "out of funds" we mean that we have no "money." By "investment funds" we mean the "sums of money" that are devoted to investment. In short, "funds" is a synonym for what is also called "money" or "currency," or what in this book is called *media of payment*.

The community's media of payment consist of the totality of coin, note currency and deposit currency in existence in the community. Coins are used only as small change in the United States, and account for only about one per cent of all media of payment. Note currency makes up about 20 per cent of the total, and the rest—about 80 per cent—consists of deposit currency. For purposes of the present discussion we can leave out of consideration the quantitatively unimportant coins and center our attention on note currency and, especially, on deposit currency. What is the nature of these media of payment and how do they come into existence?

a) Note currency and deposit currency

With the exception of some government note issues, note currency consists of *bank notes* issued by commercial banks.

Bank notes are the banks' promises to pay; they are credit instruments emitted by commercial banks.[3]

Deposit currency consists of *demand deposits* with commercial banks, i.e., deposits against which the depositor may draw checks. Other kinds of deposits—saving deposits and time deposits—cannot be regarded as media of payment because the depositor may be required to give the bank thirty days' notice before being allowed to draw against them; and in any case he may not draw *checks* against them. The essential characteristic of demand deposits is that checks may be drawn against them. In fact, a demand deposit may be defined as *a right granted by a commercial bank to a person (or corporation, government, etc.) to draw checks up to an indicated amount* (the amount of the deposit).

Checks, like bank notes, are credit instruments. Checks are drafts on commercial banks, payable on demand. These demand drafts are what we use in making payments; they are our principal media of payment. Hence one may speak of them as *check* currency instead of *deposit* currency. The check, however, is merely a device by which the payer transfers to the payee a demand deposit in the amount indicated on the check. The terms *check currency* and *deposit currency* may be used as synonyms.

It should be noted that demand deposits are not something that the community hands over to the commercial banks, but something that these banks give or "emit" to the community, in much the same way as they emit bank notes. The term "demand deposit" is unfortunately misleading. It would be more appropriate to speak of "checking rights" or "promises to honor checks." Such terminology would bring out more clearly the basic similarity between bank notes and demand deposits. Both are promises to pay, issued (or "emitted") by commercial banks,

3. The right of note issue today is almost everywhere restricted to a special type of commercial banks, the so-called "central banks." In the United States, the 12 Federal Reserve banks are the central banks. Of a total of $29,259 million of note currency in circulation in the United States on April 30, 1960, $26,695 million was issued by the Federal Reserve banks, and $2,564 by the United States Treasury.

and used by the community as media of payment. The creation or "emission" of media of payment is the main function and purpose of commercial banks; and this function distinguishes commercial banks from all other banks. Commercial banks are "banks of emission."

b) How do commercial banks create media of payment?

Commercial banks create media of payment by making loans or acquiring securities. They issue their own promises, which then circulate as media of payment, in exchange for other promises which are *not* used as media of payment. For example, when a commercial bank "makes a loan" to a firm, it takes the firm's promissory note and in exchange gives the firm a demand deposit. It merely substitutes its own promise for the firm's promise. By so doing the commercial bank supplies the firm with credit of high circulation power which enables the firm to obtain the goods and services it wants. The same process takes place when commercial banks buy bonds or other securities. The commercial banks pay for the securities by giving the seller a demand deposit. Since bonds are promises to pay, and demand deposits are also promises to pay, this transaction again involves merely an exchange of promises and the substitution of high-powered for low-powered credit.

To sum up: "funds" are media of payment; they are a form of credit possessing high circulation power. "Funds" are emitted by commercial banks in exchange for the promises to pay of individuals, corporations, and governments.

Let us next examine the connection between "funds" (i.e., media of payment) and saving, and between "funds" and investment.

"Funds" and "saving"

The popular view is that when people save, they find themselves with more "funds"—more "money" in their pockets or under the mattress or in the bank. The "money" so saved is thought of as "savings"; and the more people save, the larger, presumably, is the volume of "funds." Saving is thus thought to create "funds."

This view is wrong on several counts:

1. Saving is not the same as savings.

One confusion which obscures the relation between "funds" and saving arises from failure to distinguish *saving* from *savings*. *Saving*, the present participle of *to save*, refers to a decision which people make, or to something they do, with respect to their income. *Savings* is a noun referring to the things which people have accumulated as a result of having saved. In the phrase *saving and investment* it is the *act* of saving which is referred to. It is the counterpart of *investment*, which also refers to an action, namely the act of incurring costs in making additions to capital. On the other hand, *savings*, the result of saving, would be the counterpart of *capital*, the result of investment.

Although *savings* may consist of "funds" (see 3, below), *saving* never could. Yet the widespread habit of identifying saving with savings leads to the further identification of saving with "funds."

2. Saving means: to refrain from consuming; not: to accumulate "funds."

On Keynes's definition of *saving* (see Chapter VI, page 54), it is impossible to "save money." Saving means: not consuming one's income. Saving is something one does (or does *not* do) with *income*: it is not something one does with "money" or "funds," i.e., media of payment. This, indeed, is not only Keynes's meaning of *saving*, but is what is usually meant by people who speak of "saving money." Such terminology reflects the popular confusion of income with "money," (i.e., media of payment). In ordinary conversation this confusion may be harmless, but it is hopeless when allowed to intrude into an analysis of the saving process.

3. "Funds" may be savings for individuals, but not for a community.

An individual who saves may accumulate media of payment.

To him these media of payment constitute his *savings,* in the same way that his saving bonds, securities, and in fact all his assets constitute his savings (or the savings of those from whom he may have inherited these assets). But an individual may also increase his media of payment and other assets without saving (or inheriting the savings of others). He can do so by increasing his indebtedness. He may even *dis*save and at the same time increase his holdings of media of payment and other assets.

For the community as a whole "funds" (i.e., media of payment), created within the community and held within the community never constitute savings because whereas such "funds" are assets from the point of view of their owners, they are at the same time liabilities of the banks which created the "funds." The net asset value, for the entire community, of "funds"(or of any debts and claims) created and held within that community must, therefore, always be zero. Savings of the community can only take the form of real assets—buildings, machines, inventories—and of claims against other communities.

4. "Funds" are created by banks, not by saving.

As was shown earlier, "funds" are created by the commercial banks in exchanging their own promises to pay for the promises of individuals, firms, etc. Saving has nothing to do with the creation of "funds." If the community wants more "funds" and the banks are willing to provide them, the quantity of "funds" will increase even if no one saves. Conversely, the quantity of "funds" may decrease even though people save.

"Funds" and investment

Even as people often speak of "saving their money," so they speak of "investing their money." The idea that what is invested is "money" or "funds" is incorporated by some authors in their definitions of investment as the "commitment of funds to the purchase of income yielding assets" or the "commitment of funds to the enlargement of capital."

This view, too, like its counterpart idea that people "save money," contains several fallacies:

1. "Funds" cannot be invested.

Keynes defined investment as the "addition to the value of the capital equipment which has resulted from the productive activity of the period." If investment is understood in this sense, as referring to the process of capital formation, then it is incorrect to say that we invest "money" or "funds." We invest labor and materials. Factories are built by workmen using steel and cement, not by "funds," or by "money." "Money," or "funds," cannot be invested any more than they can be saved or consumed. It is true that an individual or firm acquiring a capital asset usually parts with "funds" in order to acquire it. But "funds" are merely the media of payment used to pay for anything one buys, not only for the purchase of a capital asset, but for consumption as well.

2. "Investment funds" are not different from other "funds."

The expression "investment funds" implies that these are different from other "funds." The expression also suggests that there is a limited amount of "investment funds" at any given time; and that this amount can be increased only by saving.

The vague and confusing term "investment funds" may mean one of two things:

a. "funds" offered in exchange for securities. In the language of the financial community the term "investment" sometimes means the purchase of securities and sometimes the securities themselves. Investment in this sense has nothing to do with investment in the economists' sense of capital formation.

b. "funds" used to pay for the production of additional capital, i.e., for labor and materials used in producing additional capital equipment.

But whether used in one sense or another, "investment funds" are no different from "funds" used to pay for other things—taxes, insurance premiums or the weekly milk bill. Like all "funds," they consist of credit instruments created by commercial banks and used by the community as media of payment. A firm needing "funds" to finance an investment need not get these "funds" from savers; it may get them by borrowing from a bank, even as consumers may borrow to finance their consumption expenditures.

3. Investment can be made without "funds."

Not only is it fallacious to think of investment as being possible only if "investment funds" are available; it is also fallacious to think that an investor must necessarily have any "funds" whatever in order to make an investment.

An investment is made whenever costs are incurred for the purpose of increasing capital. These costs may be incurred before they have to be paid and before "funds" become available to pay them. It is also possible that the costs are incurred without any "funds" ever being used to pay them. This happens for instance when a farmer engages his neighbors to help him put up a barn and compensates them by rendering similar services to them; or by giving them some of his produce in exchange. A well-known aircraft corporation, in the difficult days of its infancy, compensated workers in part by giving them stock in the corporation. When such methods are employed, no "funds" whatever are needed to carry out an investment.

Conclusion regarding "investment funds"

Having explored the meaning of "funds" and their relation to saving and investment, we come to the following conclusions:

1. "Funds" is a synonym for media of payment.
2. Media of payment are created by commercial banks in whatever quantities the community requires.
3. Saving does not create "funds." The quantity of media of payment may decline when people save more; it may increase when people save less.
4. "Funds" cannot be invested.
5. Media of payment are used to make payments, whether these payments are made for consumption or for additions to capital. There are no separate "investment funds."
6. Investment expenditures are not limited by the availability of media of payment.

SUMMARY

The important point made by Keynes is that the amounts we save depend on our income, and our income depends on investment. Hence I determines S. This is true, though only on Keynes's assumptions and definitions. The widely held notion that investment is possible only if "investment funds" have been made available by people who "saved money" is wrong. The "funds" needed for investment or for any other expenditures are created by the commercial banks. Saving has nothing to do with "funds."

Chapter Fourteen

Wages and Employment

In the early 1930's one of the great controversies among economists revolved around the question of the connection between wages[1] and the volume of employment. The "classical" view on this question was presented in the *Theory of Unemployment* by A. C. Pigou, one of Keynes's colleagues and former teachers at Cambridge. Keynes challenged the classical view and formulated a new theory of wages and employment.

THE CLASSICAL THEORY OF WAGES AND EMPLOYMENT

According to the classical theory, the amount of labor employed is determined by the demand for labor and the supply of labor. Here again, demand and supply must be understood to mean schedules or functions, as explained in Chapter III. The relation between the demand for labor and the supply of labor is shown graphically in Diagram 6. The demand for labor, designated by the symbol DL, is the schedule or function showing the amounts of labor that employers want to hire at

1. Keynes used the term *wages* in the customary sense of wage *rates*. This is the sense in which the term is used here.

Th wage *rate* is the wage per unit of labor, e. g., an hour's labor or a day's labor (time rate) or the wage per unit of the product (piece rate).

Wage rates (or wages) must be differentiated from the (weekly or annual) *earnings* of the wage earner and from *payrolls,* which are the sum of wage payments made by employers. Wage rates may fall, and yet earnings may rise because workers put in more hours or days of work; and while earnings may increase, payrolls may fall off because fewer people are employed.

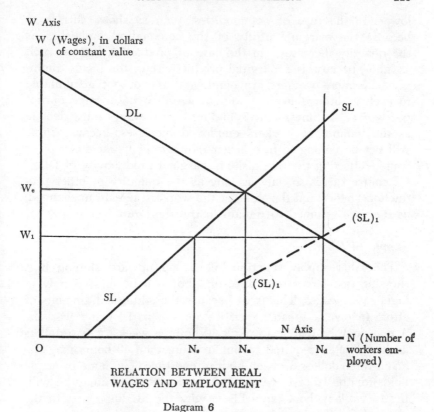

RELATION BETWEEN REAL
WAGES AND EMPLOYMENT

Diagram 6

various wages; while the supply of labor, SL, shows the quantities of labor that will be offered at these various wages. Wages are here expressed in dollars of constant value. In other words, it is the *real* wages rather than the *money* wages (also called *nominal* wages) that matter.

Demand for labor

The demand for labor is shown by a line that slopes downward because—as in the case of all things that are bought and sold—the lower the price, the larger, other things remaining equal, will be the quantity demanded. Differently stated, larger quantities will be bought only on condition that the price be lower. In the case of commodities, such as shoes, this is so because the marginal utility of the commodity diminishes as the quantity increases;[2] in the case of production factors, such as labor, because the marginal productivity of the factor diminishes. As more workers are employed[3] the output attributable to each additional worker, and hence also the average output per worker, declines. Correspondingly, real wages must decline as the number of workers employed increases, because firms will not be willing to hire larger numbers of workers except at wages reflecting the diminishing marginal productivity of labor. Of course this is so only as long as the quantity of other production factors, and the skills of the workers, remain unchanged, as they are assumed to remain in the short run.

Supply of labor

The labor supply function, SL, is an upward sloping line, showing that larger quantities of labor will be offered only at higher real wages. This is so because the additional amounts of effort involve a greater sacrifice on the part of the workers. A man may be willing to work 40 hours a week for two dollars an hour, but if required to put in more than 40 hours may demand three dollars for each hour of overtime. The same principle holds for the labor force as a whole. Some people may be willing to work without pay—this is why the SL line starts to the right of O. Most people will work only if they get paid, some being satisfied with low wages, others insisting on higher wages. A few people will take jobs only if wages are far above their actual level.

At any wage level there will be someone just barely willing to work at that wage, but not willing to work for one penny less. The wage is just high enough to overcome the disinclination

2. The marginal utility, it will be remembered, is the utility of the last added unit. One pair of shoes may be an urgent necessity and hence possess great utility. A second pair may be a convenience, a third pair rarely used, while a fourth may only clutter up the clothes closet and have no utility for its owner.

3. More correctly, this should read "as more units of labor are employed . . ." A "unit of labor" is here equated to "a worker" merely for brevity and convenience.

to work, or the *disutility of labor*, of this marginal worker. The next worker, with a somewhat stronger disinclination to work, will take a job only if (real) wages were raised just enough to overcome his disinclination. Then *he* would become the marginal worker. The greater the number of people employed, the higher will be the disutility of labor to the marginal worker, or the *marginal disutility of labor*, and the higher therefore must be the real wage.

Determinants of the volume of employment

According to the classical theory, the amount of employment will always tend to correspond to the figure at which the labor demand and labor supply functions intersect. On the assumptions of our diagram, the number of people employed will be N_a. The wage at which this number of people is employed is W_e. This is the equilibrium wage. Only at that wage are demand for labor and supply of labor equal. All those who are willing to work at that wage (or at a lower wage) find employment; more cannot be employed at that wage.

How can employment be increased according to the classical theory?

The question now arises: how could aggregate employment be increased beyond N_a? According to the classical theory there is only one way to increase employment: workers must be willing to accept lower real wages. If the labor supply function in Diagram 6 were shifted to $(SL)_1$, indicating a willingness on the part of workers to accept lower wages for given amounts of labor, or to supply more work at given wages, then employment would promptly expand to N_d.

Since it is notoriously difficult to persuade workers to accept wage cuts, could any other methods be used to increase employment? Could an increase in employment be brought about, for instance, through an increase in aggregate demand for goods? The classical economists said No. An increase in aggregate demand for goods does not mean that the productivity of labor is also increased. The labor demand function which is based on the marginal productivity of labor, would be unchanged. If firms wanted to employ more labor, say N_d, to meet the increased aggregate demand for goods, they would have to reduce wages from W_e to W_1. But at a wage of W_1 the quantity of labor forthcoming would be only N_s. To get more workers, employers would have to raise wages again. When wages are back to W_e, employment will again be at N_a, exactly where we started from. Nothing can be gained, therefore, from an increase in the aggregate demand for goods. Reductions in wages are the only way to increase employment.

In the depression years of the early 1930's the classical theory of wages and employment was regarded as self-evident by most economists and especially by employers, since it rationalized their natural desire to cut wages. They attributed unemployment to unreasonable wage demands on the part of workers. Excessive wages had brought on the depression, they said. The only short cut to prosperity, they claimed, was a wage cut.

KEYNES'S CRITICISM OF CLASSICAL WAGE THEORY

Though the wage cuts were promptly put into effect, depression and unemployment continued and worsened. Keynes showed why. He exposed the errors in the classical theory and pointed out the way to recovery and full employment.

The classical theory of wages, as developed by Pigou, was based on two postulates,[4] said Keynes. *The first postulate of classical wage theory states that the wage tends to equal the marginal product of labor.* This, as we have already seen, is the principle underlying the demand for labor. Firms tend to employ labor up to the point at which the addition to the product attributable to the last added worker is just equal to the wage. Obviously no firm employing workers to produce goods for sale will hire a worker unless it expects him to produce enough to cover at least his own wage. On the other hand, the firm will want to hire additional workers as long as each additional

4. A postulate is a proposition which is taken for granted as self-evident, and which forms the first premise in a train of reasoning.

worker employed adds more to the firm's output than his wage, Keynes saw nothing wrong with this first postulate of classical wage theory and specifically affirmed his acceptance of it.

The second postulate of classical wage theory states that the wage tends to equal the marginal disutility of labor. This means that the wage prevailing at any moment is just sufficient to secure the amount of labor actually employed at that moment; that if the wage were lowered, some workers—those just barely willing to work at the prevailing wage—would quit their jobs; and, conversely, that additional workers could be found only if wages were increased. This principle, it will be remembered, explains the supply of labor.

Fallacies underlying the second postulate of classical wage theory

Keynes challenged this second postulate of classical wage theory. The real wage, he said, rarely equals the marginal disutility of labor. At most times there are numbers of workers willing and anxious to work at prevailing wages, but unable to find employment. In fact, workers may remain unemployed despite a willingness on their part to accept *lower* real wages.

It should not be thought that this situation can be blamed on the action and policies of labor unions. The view that labor unions set wages too high to permit employment of all potential workers, and that they perpetuate unemployment by their resistance to wage cuts, contains two fallacies, said Keynes.

a) Labor unions bargain for money wages, not real wages

1. The first fallacy is the idea that labor unions bargain for *real* wages. Labor unions bargain for *money* wages, not for real wages. Furthermore, they are more interested in money wages than in real wages. Each union is eager to secure for its member money wages that are high in comparison with the money wages of other workers. Unions are less concerned with the level of real wages which changes with fluctuations in consumers' goods prices and affects all wage earners alike. Of

course, when prices rise, and the level of real wages is lowered as a result, this may be seized upon by unions as an argument for demanding a wage increase. But still, the demand is for higher money wages for the particular group of workers, and the higher money wages may or may not mean higher real wages, depending on whether prices rise more or less than wages.

Workers will often refuse to work if faced with a cut in their money wages, or if they are refused an increase in money wages. A refusal to work for less than a specified money wage is, however, not at all the same as a refusal to work for a lower real wage. Workers may strike if their money wages are reduced from $100 a week to $95, but they may accept without protest a cut in real wages resulting from an increase in the consumer price index from 100 to 105, while their money wages remain unchanged at $100.

When workers are willing to accept reductions in their real wages brought about by price increases, we are justified in concluding that the real wage before the rise in prices was higher than the minimum real wage the workers were willing to accept. The real wage, then, exceeded the marginal disutility of labor. This is the usual situation. Only in full employment is the real wage equal to the marginal disutility of labor. If full employment prevails, then, indeed, additional workers can be found only on condition that real wages be raised. In fact, Keynes defined full employment as a situation in which the wage is equal to the marginal disutility of labor.

b) Money wage bargains do not affect real wages

2. The second fallacy in the classical wage theory is the idea that the wage bargains which determine the level of money wages also determine the level of real wages. Even if workers did want to bargain for *real* wages, it would not be in their power to do so, said Keynes. The real wage, which must equal the marginal product of labor, depends on the quantity of labor employed. The quantity of labor which firms employ depends on the quantity of output they decide to produce. This, in turn,

depends on the aggregate demand for goods. If aggregate demand for goods is such that the number of workers employed is N_a, then real wages will be W_e. (See Diagram 6.) Of course, if this real wage were not sufficiently high to induce N_a workers to accept jobs, then real wages would have to be higher and fewer people would be employed. If a real wage of W_e were just sufficient to induce N_a workers to accept jobs, then full employment would prevail. But if a wage of W_e were more than sufficient to call forth a quantity N_a of labor, then some workers must be involuntarily unemployed. Despite their willingness to work for less than the prevailing wage, they are unable to get jobs.

It is not true, in other words, that the volume of employment and the real wage are determined by the intersection of the labor demand function with the labor supply function. The volume of employment, as was shown in Chapter II, is determined by the aggregate demand for goods; and, with a given labor demand function, the real wage is determined by the volume of employment. The labor supply function indicates only the *maximum* quantity of labor which will be forthcoming at various real wages; or the *minimum* real wages that are required to call forth various quantities of labor. The quantity of labor actually employed is usually smaller than the maximum available at prevailing real wages; and the prevailing real wages are usually higher than the minimum required to call forth the actual volume of employment. Only in full employment do actual employment and real wages coincide with these maximums and minimums.

Thus, if the labor supply function is SL, then N_a constitutes full employment and W_e is the equilibrium wage. But if the labor supply function were $(SL)_1$, N_a would be less than maximum, or full, employment, and W_e would be more than the minimum, or equilibrium, real wage required to secure N_a workers. Only if employment were N_d, and real wages consequently W_1, would full employment and equilibrium wages prevail. But there is no reason to expect that employment would increase to N_d merely because the workers are willing to accept a real wage as low as W_1.

Results of cuts in money wages

What would happen if workers agreed to wage cuts all around in an effort to reduce real wages and thus to expand employment? Of course the actual cutting could be done only in money wages. The result of cuts in money wages is to reduce the workers' money incomes. With lower money incomes the aggregate demand for goods will decline, i.e., the community will be willing to spend less for given quantities of goods than it was willing to spend before. But, offsetting this decline in aggregate demand, there will be an increase in the aggregate supply of goods. Because the wage reductions lowered the money costs of production, firms are willing to offer given quantities of output for smaller proceeds than before. Goods will be offered at lower prices. As a result, the quantity of goods bought and sold remains (practically) unchanged, output and employment are (practically) unchanged, but money wages, incomes, and prices, will all be lower. Since prices decline in the same proportion as money wages, real wages are (practically) unaffected. According to Keynes, then, wage cuts are a self-defeating maneuver and are useless as a device to increase employment.

HOW EMPLOYMENT CAN BE INCREASED

The only way in which employment can be increased is through an increase in the aggregate demand for goods, said Keynes. An increase in aggregate demand would tend to raise prices, making it profitable for firms to expand output, unless the entire price increase is absorbed by higher wages. Wages, however, are not likely to increase as fast as prices in periods of economic recovery and expansion. In other words, real wages decline. But since workers—those employed as well as those unemployed—are willing to work for less than the previously prevailing real wages, employment expands in response to the increase in the aggregate demand for goods. This process of expansion can go on until there are no more workers willing to work for less than the prevailing real wages or even for as much as the prevailing real wages. Only when this point, i.e., full employment, is reached are further increases in aggregate demand for goods unable to increase employment. Only then does the classical theory apply.

SUMMARY OF KEYNES'S THEORY OF WAGES AND EMPLOYMENT

The theory of wages and employment development by Keynes and outlined in the preceding pages of this chapter is summarized in the following ten points:

1. Wage bargains always refer to money (or nominal) wages, not to real wages.
2. Workers or unions of workers are unable to bargain for real wages, even if they wanted to do so.
3. Real wages depend on the marginal productivity of the quantity of labor employed.
4. The quantity of labor employed depends on the demand for goods.
5. Though workers may refuse to work for a lower money wage, they do not necessarily refuse to work for a lower real wage.
6. Except in full employment, the real wage exceeds the marginal disutility of labor. This means that there are unemployed workers who would be willing to work at prevailing real wages or less, if they could find employment. (Denial of second postulate of classical wage theory.)
7. Full employment is defined as a situation in which there are no such involuntarily unemployed people; prevailing wages then are equal to the marginal disutility of labor.
8. Reductions in money wages can not increase the volume of employment, but only cause prices and incomes to fall.
9. When aggregate demand for goods increases (under conditions of less than full employment), employment increases too.
10. An increase in employment, in the short run, must be associated with a decline in real wages. (Affirmation of first postulate of classical wage theory.)

THE PIGOU EFFECT

Keynes's argument in the *General Theory*, as mentioned earlier, was largely directed against Pigou's contention that employment could be increased only by cutting wages. It seems that Pigou was at least partly convinced by Keynes, for in his *Lapses from Full Employment* Pigou conceded that the problem of unemployment could be better attacked by manipulating aggregate demand than by manipulating wages. This was a surrender to Keynes on the principal point of the controversy.[5] Pigou's conversion, however, was reluctant at best. He continued to maintain that in most situations "thoroughgoing competition among wage earners would ensure the establishment and maintenance of full employment."[6]

One of the arguments which Pigou advanced in support of his view has received much attention, also from the followers of Keynes. When wages fall, and prices consequently also fall, the relative value of assets with a fixed money value (such as bonds, savings deposits, or media of payment) correspondingly rises. The owners of these assets are richer as a result of the decline in prices. Being richer, they increase their consumption. Aggregate demand for goods, and hence employment, rise; and the rise in employment is a result of the wage reduction which was the first link in the whole chain of causation. This effect of changes in wages on employment via changes in the relative value of assets has come to be known as the *Pigou effect*.

Keynes himself did not consider the Pigou effect. It is questionable if this effect has much quantitative importance. We know little about the extent to which changes in aggregate demand are attributable to changes in the relative value of assets with fixed money values. But it is fairly certain that other factors, especially changes in income, have a far greater influence on aggregate demand for goods, and hence on employment, than has the Pigou effect.

5. Cf. Dillard, *The Economics of John Maynard Keynes*, p. 24.
6. Pigou, *Lapses from Full Employment*, p. 25.

EFFECTS OF REDUCTIONS IN MONEY WAGES

While Pigou had to revise his theory of wages and employment in the light of the Keynesian theory, Keynes in his turn allowed some validity to the classical theory. In fact, Keynes did not give a dogmatic answer to the question of the actual effects of changes in money wages on employment. Many different effects are possible, he said. In every case the question must be: how do changes in wages affect the aggregate demand for goods? A reduction in money wages, said Keynes, will have the following effects:

1. It will change the distribution of income in favor of the rentier class. Since the latter includes the richer members of the community whose marginal propensity to consume is low, this will probably reduce the aggregate demand for goods. (This is not to be confused with the above-mentioned Pigou effect which refers to changes in distribution of wealth rather than to changes in the distribution of income.)
2. It may stimulate exports, i.e., foreign demand for goods.
3. It will, however, at the same time worsen the terms of trade (i.e., the amount of goods that must be exported to pay for imports). This reduces the real income of the community. At a lower income a greater proportion of income will be consumed.
4. It may lead to expectations of further wage cuts, in which case aggregate demand would fall off, as investors and consumers would postpone their expenditures until prices have fallen further.
5. It will reduce the need for media of payment to transact business and will consequently cause interest rates to fall. This may stimulate investment and hence increase aggregate demand.
6. It may produce optimism among employers, but may also lead to labor trouble. The former would tend to increase, the latter to decrease, aggregate demand.

7. It will increase the real burden of debts, which will tend to make businessmen pessimistic and hence decrease the inducement to invest and thus reduce aggregate demand.

In sum, reductions in money wages have all sorts of effects. Most of these, however, are not of a nature to increase aggregate demand. Hence there is no justification for relying on wage cuts to bring about an increase in employment; they may well have the effect of decreasing it.

Chapter Fifteen

The Theory of Interest

THE NATURE OF INTEREST

Theories of interest explain the nature of interest and the determinants of the rate of interest.[1] Keynes explained interest as a phenomenon of *liquidity preference*. He said that people generally prefer to hold their wealth in liquid form, and that they will not hold it in non-liquid form unless they get a reward for doing so. This reward is called interest. Interest, he said, is "the reward for parting with liquidity for a specified time" (167). Keynes's theory of interest is known as the *liquidity preference* theory of interest.

Meaning of "liquidity"

"Liquidity" here means: assets in a form which enables the owner to exchange them at once for other forms of wealth. Some assets are "liquid," others are not. Houses, jewelry, art objects, are things that cannot be readily exchanged for other things and are therefore considered highly illiquid. Commodities traded on organized exchanges, such as wheat or sugar, and stocks and bonds traded in organized security markets, are more liquid. But the one asset which is completely liquid is "money," i.e., media of payment. In fact, Keynes used the term "liquidity" as a synonym for "money" (media of payment); and the "liquidity preference" theory of interest could as easily, and more

1. There are many interest rates, reflecting differences in the length of time for which loans are made, degrees of risk of default, degrees of monopolistic elements in the markets for particular types of loans, legal restrictions, and custom. Following a well established tradition in interest theory, Keynes disregarded these differences and assumed that there is only one rate of interest.

unambiguously, be called the "money preference" or "media of payment preference" theory of interest.

Interest is the price which equilibrates desire for media of payment with available quantity of media of payment

If there were enough media of payment to satisfy everybody's preference for liquidity, nobody would need to be given a reward for parting with liquidity. But there are not enough media of payment. For this reason people must be induced— by the prospect of a reward in the form of interest—to curtail their desire for "cash" (media of payment) sufficiently to bring this desire into balance with the limited quantity of media of payment available. Interest may therefore also be defined as "the 'price' which equilibrates the desire to hold wealth in the form of cash with the available quantity of cash" (167).

Motives for liquidity

Why should people want to hold or "store" their wealth in the form of media of payment—a form of wealth which yields no income—in preference to storing it in the form of income-yielding assets? At first blush, this preference, as Keynes himself pointed out, seems "insane." Yet people do want to hold media of payment. Why? For what reason or purpose? Keynes listed four motives which induce people to want to hold media of payment:

1. *The income motive.* People must hold media of payment "to bridge the interval between the receipt of income and its disbursement" (195). How much media of payment a person will hold, on an average, for this purpose, depends on the size of his income and on the frequency of income payment. A person who gets $60 paid out to him each week may perhaps hold, on an average, as much as $30, or half a week's pay, starting each week with $60 and ending it with an empty purse. If the same person were paid $3000 once a year and wanted to spend this income evenly over the year, he would have to hold, on an average $1500, equal to half a year's income.

2. *The business motive.* For similar reasons business firms must hold media of payment. How much, will depend on the dollar volume of business and on the regularity or irregularity of receipts and disbursement.

3. *The precautionary motive.* In addition to the amounts of media of payment which people and firms require to bridge the gap between income and expenditures, they may also want to keep media of payment to meet future liabilities and to enable them to cover unforeseen expenditures arising from sudden emergencies or from bargain opportunities.

4. *The speculative motive.* People and firms want to hold media of payment when they expect the rate of interest to rise in the future. If this expectation should turn out to be correct, media of payment could be lent out more advantageously at the future date, or debts (e.g., bonds) bought more cheaply. Of course the future movements of the interest rate are uncertain; and to act on the assumption that it will rise (i.e., that the prices of bonds and other debts will fall) is to speculate. It is because of this that the desire to hold media of payment for this purpose is said to spring from the "speculative motive."

DETERMINATION OF THE RATE OF INTEREST

The answer to the first question of interest theory: What is interest? has already, in part, supplied the answer to the second question of interest theory: What are the determinants of the rate of interest? If interest is "the price which equilibrates the desire to hold . . . cash with the available quantity of cash," then the rate of interest must be determined by the interaction between the demand for "cash" (media of payment) and the supply of "cash."

Demand for media of payment

The demand for media of payment may be defined as *the schedule of quantities of media of payment the community wants to hold at various rates of interest.* This schedule Keynes called the *liquidity preference schedule,* or *liquidity preference function,* designated by the letter L. Below is an example of a (hypothetical) liquidity preference schedule:

Diagram 7 shows the liquidity preference function graphically.

As pointed out above, in the section on *Motives for liquidity*; liquidity preference, or the demand for media of payment, springs from four motives—income, business, precaution, and speculation. The first three of these may be lumped together as giving rise to a demand for media of payment for use in transactions,[2] while the fourth motive gives rise to a demand for media of payment to hoard. Translating this into the terminology of traditional monetary theory, the demand for "money" springs partly from the function of "money" as a medium of exchange (transactions) and partly from its function as a store of wealth (hoarding). While pre-Keynesian monetary economists did not fail to point out that "money is a store of

TABLE 8

Liquidity Preference Schedule

if the rate of interest is	the community may want to hold media of payment in the amount of
10%	70 billion dollars
6%	125 " "
3%	175 " "
2 ½%	200 " "
2%	unlimited

2. Keynes combined only the first two motives—income and business—into what he called the "transactions motive," continuing to differentiate between the "transactions motive" and the "precautionary motive," but lumped these two motives together in analysing the demand for media of payment springing from them. It is simpler to regard the "precautionary motive" as being part of the "transactions motive." Media of payment held for "precautionary" reasons are to be used to meet expected future debt payments, usually arising from *past transactions,* and unexpected future payments, arising from *future transactions.* There is therefore no special need to differentiate between "transactions motive" and "precautionary motive."

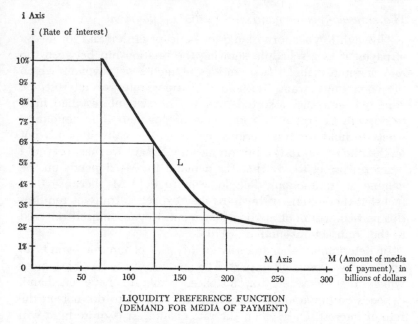

LIQUIDITY PREFERENCE FUNCTION
(DEMAND FOR MEDIA OF PAYMENT)

Diagram 7

wealth" in addition to being a medium of exchange, they neglected to take account of the "store of wealth" function in their analysis of the demand for media of payment. They attributed this demand exclusively to the "medium of exchange" function. Keynes called attention to the significant difference between the transactions demand (L_1) and the hoarding, or speculative, demand (L_2) for media of payment.

The total amount of media of payment (M) is held partly for transactions purposes and partly for speculative purposes. The part of M which is held for transactions purposes is designated as M_1, the part which is held for speculative purposes is designated as M_2. Correspondingly, the demand (L) for media of payment (M) must be segregated into two components: L_1 is the demand for M_1, and L_2 is the demand for M_2. These two components of L are largely independent of one another and are differently determined.

The transactions demand for media of payment

Although Keynes formulated the concept of demand for media of payment as a schedule showing the relationship between the rate of interest and the quantities of media of payment which the community wants to hold at various rates of interest, he admitted—or rather asserted—that the rate of interest had little to do with the quantities of media of payment the community wants to hold for transactions purposes. L_1 really depends not on the rate of interest, i, but on income, Y, said Keynes. It would be more correct to say that the demand for M_1 depends on the volume of transactions. People want to hold M_1 because they feel that the volume of business they expect to transact requires this particular sum of media of payment. Keynes himself referred to the "transactions-motive" (170).

In determining the quantity of M_1 the community wants to hold, i plays a negligible part. The amount of media of payment which a storekeeper, for instance, wants to have on hand, depends on the amount of business he expects to do, not on the rate of interest. Only when the rate of interest is quite high will consumers and firms be induced to do with less M_1, for only then is the reward for finding ways of economizing media of payment high enough to compensate for the inconvenience of such economizing. The L_1 function, therefore, will be inelastic[3] for lower ranges of i, but somewhat elastic in higher ranges of i, as shown in Diagram 8.

The speculative demand for media of payment

Unlike the demand for M_1 which depends chiefly on Y and is unresponsive to changes in i, the demand for M_2 is highly

3. Elasticity of demand expresses the relation between a change in quantity demanded and the corresponding change in price. If a change in price results in no change whatever in quantity demanded, the demand is totally inelastic for this price range. If a 10% drop in price is associated with a 10% increase in quantity demanded, the elasticity of demand is one, or "unit elasticity." When elasticity is less than one, demand is said to be relatively inelastic; when elasticity is greater than one, demand is said to be relatively elastic.

sensitive to changes in i. The chief reason why people want to
"hoard money," i.e., to hold M_2, is that they expect interest-
bearing assets to decline in value, or, what comes to the same
thing, that they expect the rate of interest to rise. If a bond
yielding $4 interest a year is selling for $100 today, and if I
believe that I could buy that same bond next month for $90,
it would be advantageous for me to forego the 4% interest income (34 cents per month) I could get by buying the bond
today and to hold media of payment until I can get the bond
for $90, at which price it would yield about 4½% interest. If
next month I continue to expect the future price of the bond to
be lower, i.e., the interest rate to be higher, I would continue to

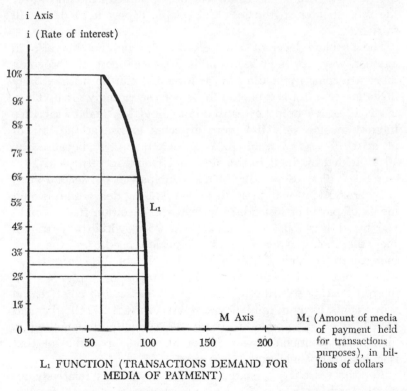

i Axis

i (Rate of interest)

L_1 FUNCTION (TRANSACTIONS DEMAND FOR
MEDIA OF PAYMENT)

Diagram 8

hold non-interest-bearing media of payment. Only when I
believe that the rate of interest is about to decline would I part
with media of payment and acquire interest-bearing securities.
L_2 (the speculative demand for media of payment), then, depends on the relationship between present and expected future
rates of interest. The more general the expectation of a rise in i,
and the more confidently this expectation is held, the greater
will be the demand for M_2.

Though it is the difference between present and expected
rates of interest, rather than the actual level of i, which is
relevant to L_2, the absolute level of i has some bearing on
expected future i. At high rates of interest the expectation that
the rate will rise still further will be weakened; and the lower
the rate of interest, the less will people expect it to drop still
further.

The absolute level of i affects the demand for M_2 also in
another way. At high rates of interest the cost of foregoing
interest income by holding M_2 is high and can be justified only
if the increase in i is expected to be correspondingly great. Thus,
if i is 10%, it would be justifiable to hold M_2, and to sacrifice
interest income, only if i were expected to rise at the rate of
at least 10% (i.e., from 10% to 11%) a year; because the
10% yielded by debts in the first year would in turn yield 10%
—or 1% (.10 × .10 = .01)of the principal—in the second year.
If i were 50%, it would pay to forego holding debts, and to hold
media of payment instead, only in the expectation that i would
rise by at least 50%—i.e., to at least 75%—within a year. On
the other hand, when i is 2%, a person needs to expect an
increase in i of only 4/100 of 1% (i.e., 2% of 2%) in order to
justify him in holding media of payment in preference to
interest-bearing securities. This, said Keynes, is the chief reason
why i is not likely to fall below 2%. At a rate of 2% the demand
for M_2 is almost perfectly elastic—the community is willing to
absorb all additional quantities of M_2 made available at that
rate because people expect i to rise.

For the reasons just stated, the L_2 function is relatively inelastic for high values of i, and almost perfectly elastic for low
values of i, as shown in Diagram 9.

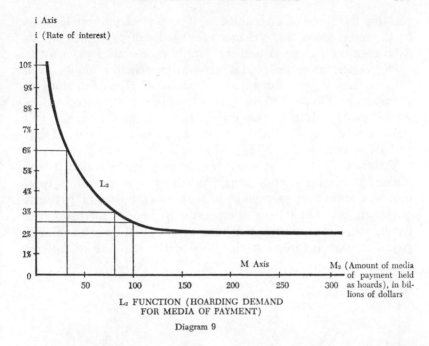

L₂ FUNCTION (HOARDING DEMAND
FOR MEDIA OF PAYMENT)

Diagram 9

Supply of media of payment

The supply of media of payment is the schedule which shows how much M the creators of M—the commercial banks—are willing to create at various levels of the rate of interest. The ability of the commercial banks to create M is generally thought to be regulated and limited by their reserves; and the size of the reserves of commercial banks depends on actions of the central bank. The central bank, in turn, decides on grounds of public policy, rather than on the basis of i, how much M the community should have. Hence the supply of M is completely inelastic with respect to i, i.e., a higher i will not call forth a larger M than would a lower i. A graphic representation of the M supply function shows it as a vertical line. (See Diagram 10.)

Relations between L_1, L_2, M, and i

The analysis of the determinants of the rate of interest follows the same principles as does demand-and-supply analysis in explaining the price of a commodity. The rate of interest is given by the intersection of the demand for media of payment (liquidity preference function) and the supply of media of payment.

Distinction must be made between movements along given demand and supply functions and shifts of these functions to different positions. With a given liquidity preference, an increase in M (shift of the supply function to the right) will cause i to decrease. With a given M, an increase in L_2 (shift of L_2 function to the right) will raise i.

This last point was stressed by Keynes, who claimed it was often not correctly understood. When the people of a community decide that they want to keep more media of payment on hand, i.e., when their "propensity to hoard" increases, the result, said Keynes, is not that they actually hold more media of payment than before, but that they drive the rate of interest

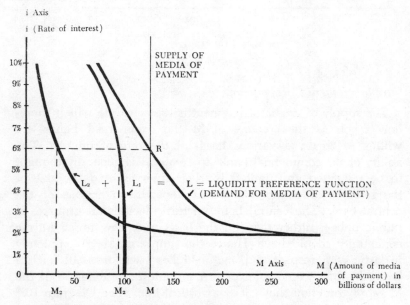

DETERMINATION OF RATE OF INTEREST BY INTERACTION
OF DEMAND FOR MEDIA OF PAYMENT (COMPOSED OF
$L_1 + L_2$) AND SUPPLY OF MEDIA OF PAYMENT

Diagram 10

higher. An increase in the actual quantity of media of payment can come about only as a result of the creation of additional media of payment by the commercial banks.

The rate of interest will also be affected by changes in the volume of transactions. An increase in the volume of transactions will raise L_1, cause a larger amount of M to be allocated to M_1, and consequently leave less M to satisfy the demand for M_2. As a result, i must rise, even though neither the quantity of media of payment nor the propensity to hoard have changed.

Diagram 10 shows how the rate of interest is determined by the interaction of the demand for and the supply of media of payment. Demand for media of payment, L, is composed of L_1 and L_2, the transactions demand and the hoarding demand for media of payment. If the quantity of media of payment (M) made available by the banks is 125 billion dollars, the supply function will intersect the liquidity preference function at a point R. The rate of interest which equates L with M at this point is 6%. When i is 6%, the community requires (according to the figures assumed in Table 8 and Diagrams 7-10) 95 billion dollars of media of payment for transactions purposes (M_1), leaving 30 billion dollars to satisfy the demand for media of payment for hoarding (M_2).

COMPARISON OF KEYNESIAN INTEREST THEORY WITH CLASSICAL INTEREST THEORY

1. The liquidity preference theory is a *monetary* interest theory. It regards interest as the price paid for holding media of payment (Keynes called it "money" or "cash")—"the 'price' which equilibrates the desire to hold . . . cash with the available quantity of cash" (167). This is in contrast to the *real* interest theory of the classical economists who regarded interest as the price paid for the use of *capital*, or the price which equilibrates the demand of capital (investment) with the supply of capital (saving).

2. According to classical interest theory, interest is the reward for *saving*, i.e., for not consuming income. Keynes pointed out that this could not be so, since a person gets no interest if he

keeps media of payment under his mattress, although he has saved just as surely as when he lends these same media of payment out at interest. Interest, said Keynes, is not the reward of not-spending; it is the reward of not-hoarding (174).

3. The classical theory holds that an increase in saving will reduce the rate of interest and thus encourage investment. According to the liquidity preference theory, interest has a bearing on investment, but saving has nothing (directly) to do with the rate of interest.

WHY KEYNES HAD TO DISPROVE THE
CLASSICAL THEORY OF INTEREST

The last point gives the clue to the importance of the position occupied by the theory of interest in the Keynesian economics. This importance may be described as negative rather than positive: it lies not so much in the positive contribution of a new and more convincing theory of interest, as it does in the negative contribution of showing the older theory wrong. Keynes had to prove the old theory wrong because unless he did so, his idea of a deficiency of aggregate demand and his whole theory of employment and output would be vitiated. Keynes argued that a decline in consumption would not be compensated by a corresponding increase in investment, but would instead diminish employment and output as a whole. This reasoning could not be accepted as valid as long as the classical theory of interest remained unchallenged. The classical theory of interest says that when people spend less on consumption, i.e., when they save more, the interest rate will be driven down to the point at which all the savings can be invested. The reduced consumption expenditures are thus compensated by increased investment expenditures, leaving total expenditures, or effective demand for goods, unchanged. On this reasoning the classical economists contended that there could never be a deficiency of effective demand. To prove their contention wrong, Keynes had to demolish the classical theory of interest. To demolish it convincingly, he necessarily had to formulate an alternative theory of interest.

THE "LOANABLE FUNDS" THEORY OF INTEREST

This theory, which has been put forward as an alternative to the liquidity preference theory, says that interest is determined by the demand for loans and the supply of "loanable funds." As Professor Abba P. Lerner pointed out,[4] this comes to practically the same thing as the liquidity preference theory. A change in the demand for loans, unless it stems from a desire on the part of the community to change the amount of media of payment in its possession, must always be offset by an equal change in the supply of loans. If the demand for loans increases because the community wants to *spend* more (and not because it wants to *hold* more M), the increased spending will cause the recipients of the additional sums expended to lend them out again. They will do this because, as a result of unanticipated receipts, they find themselves with more M than they want. The supply of loans is thus increased in consequence of the increase in the demand for loans, and in an equal degree. The rate of interest, therefore, is not affected by changes in the demand for loans for spending. Only if the increase in the demand for loans stems from a desire on the part of the community to change its *holdings* of M, will i be affected, because in that case there will be no corresponding change in the supply of loans.

Though the "loanable funds" theory thus appears almost identical with the liquidity preference theory, it may also be regarded as merely a modification of the classical theory of interest. According to the "loanable funds" theory, the supply of "loanable funds" is made up of three components: the amount of media of payment saved, the amount dishoarded, and the credit newly created by the banking system. Now, supposing dishoarding and newly created credit to be zero, the entire supply of "loanable funds" would be attributable to saving; and i would then be determined by the relation between saving and investment, as in the classical theory.[5]

---

4. Lerner, A. P. "Interest Theory–Supply and Demand for Loans or Supply and Demand for Cash" in Harris, *The New Economics.*
5. See Hansen, *A Guide to Keynes,* Chap. 7.

The identification of saving with media of payment is a weakness of the "loanable funds" theory, even as it is a weakness of the classical theory. The implication is that saving increases the quantity of media of payment. Of course it does no such thing. Any individual, when he saves, may increase his holding of M correspondingly. The community as a whole, however, can not increase its media of payment by saving. The quantity of M is always what the commercial banks—the creators of media of payment—decide to make it. Saving, so far from increasing M, is on the contrary likely to decrease it, because saving tends to decrease the volume of transactions and hence also to decrease the demands made on the commercial banks for the provision of media of payment.

Chapter Sixteen

Criticism of Keynes's Theory of Interest

Keynes's theory of interest, presented in the preceding chapter, contains some inconsistencies and contradictions. The present chapter deals with these and suggests a reformulation of the theory of interest.

INCONSISTENCIES AND CONTRADICTIONS IN KEYNES'S THEORY OF INTEREST

What is the "reward for parting with liquidity?"

Keynes said that "interest is the reward for parting with liquidity." But why regard only interest as such a reward? Why not any property income?

Interest is the income derived only from holding debts. When people part with liquidity they do not necessarily acquire debts, but may also acquire "equities," such as real estate, or stock in a corporation, or an ownership interest in an unincorporated enterprise. The income derived from owning such non-liquid assets would be rent, dividends, and profit, respectively. Any and all of these property incomes, and not only interest, may be regarded as the "reward" for holding non-liquid assets instead of liquid media of payment.

Liquidity preference theory expresses a tautology

The reason for singling out interest as the "reward for parting with liquidity" is that liquidity preference really involves only the choice between holding media of payment and holding debts, i.e., interest-bearing assets (170, footnote). A person who expects the prices of stocks or other equities to decline would presumably not want to hold his wealth in the form of such assets. But he would not necessarily want to hold media of payment instead of equities. He would want to hold either media of payment or debts. He would hold media of payment if he expected the price of debts (e.g., bonds) to fall—in other words, if he expected the rate of interest to rise; he would hold debts if he expected the price of debts to rise, i.e., the rate of interest to fall, or if he expected them to remain unchanged.

What all this comes to is simply this: people prefer to hold that type of asset which they expect to yield them the greatest increase in their wealth either in the form of income or in the form of capital gains. People prefer to hold media of payment when they believe that only in this way they can keep the money value (i.e., the value measured in dollars) of their wealth intact, whereas holding other assets would cause the money value of their wealth to shrink. People prefer holding debts to holding other assets if debts seem the most advantageous type of asset to hold. The interest income which they derive from holding debts is not the "reward for parting with liquidity," but the "reward" for holding interest-yielding assets in place of other assets. Stated in this way, the proposition is a tautology which explains nothing concerning the nature of interest and why interest is paid.

Liquidity preference should explain supply of media of payment

As formulated by Keynes, the liquidity preference theory states that interest must be paid to people as an inducement to "part with liquidity" (media of payment). Accordingly one could set up a schedule showing how much media of payment people would "part with" if the rate of interest at which they could "part with" them were, say, 2%; how much more they would "part with" if the rate of interest were 3%, 4%, and so on. Such a schedule would be a supply-of-media-of-payment schedule.

In the Keynesian theory, however, liquidity preference furnishes not the *supply*-of-media-of-payment schedule, but the *demand*-for-media-of-payment schedule. This schedule shows how much media of payment people want to *hold* if the rate of interest is, say, 10%; how much more media of payment they would want to hold if the rate of interest were 6%, 3%, and so on. Alternatively stated, the Keynesian liquidity preference function, L, shows how much interest people will pay for holding various quantities of media of payment; it does not show how much interest people must be paid for parting with media of payment.

Interest is paid for "creating" liquidity

The supply of media of payment in the Keynesian formulation is the schedule of the quantities of such media put at the disposal of the community by the commercial banks. It is they— the commercial banks—that are paid interest for furnishing "liquidity," i.e., media of payment. But when banks supply media of payment they do not "part with" liquidity; they "create" liquidity. Interest, therefore, is the "reward for *creating* liquidity," not the "reward for *parting* with liquidity."

Is the supply of media of payment inelastic?

In the Keynesian theory the supply of media of payment is regarded as inelastic with respect to the rate of interest; the M supply function is shown as a vertical line.

An absolutely inelastic M supply function implies that the quantity of media of payment made available by the banks is fixed. But the way the banking system operates, at least in the United States, is to furnish the community with all the M it wants at a given rate of interest. If the demand for M outruns the ability of the banks to create deposits on the basis of their existing reserves, the banks can, and do, borrow from the Federal Reserve banks. This means that the M supply function is perfectly interest-elastic and should be shown as a horizontal line. The idea that the banking system fixes the quantity of media of payment is contradicted by the facts and by the professed aim of the Federal Reserve System to supply an "elastic" currency, i.e., to create media of payment in response to the needs of the community.

Is there a scarcity of media of payment?

The idea that interest must be paid in order to induce people to part with media of payment implies that there are not enough media of payment to satisfy everybody's liquidity preference. Only if media of payment are scarce does it make sense to "reward" people for parting with them, i.e., for lending them to others who need them more urgently.

But why suppose that media of payment are scarce? Media of payment are created by the commercial banks in whatever quantities the community may demand. The commercial banks create media of payment when they make loans or buy securities and create their own debts in exchange for those other debts. Since the banks derive an income from the loans and securities they hold, they are anxious to hold as many of them as they can —as many, that is, as the community is offering to banks in order to get media of payment. The limit is set by the community's requirements of media of payment and by its ability to offer good securities to the banks.[1]

The banks provide all the media of payment the community demands.[2] There is no scarcity of media of payment. Consequently there is no need for the payment of interest as an inducement to owners of this "scarce commodity" to dishoard some of it. Interest, as Keynes's own analysis showed (see page 143, above) is paid to the banks—and not for "parting with liquidity" but for creating media of payment.

It might be argued that anything for which a price must be paid is scarce. But media of payment are scarce only in the same sense that marriage licenses are scarce and command a price. Marriage licenses are issued to all who are entitled to them. There is no "scarcity" of marriage licenses, even though they cost something. Similarly, media of payment are not scarce. They can be made available in any desired quantities and as

---

1. Of course the banks cannot take securities, or make loans, which they believe will not be paid on the due date.

2. This statement is not to be taken to mean that the banks can and do provide all the additional *income* people may desire. Almost everybody would like to have more "money" as a gift, but this is not the same as wanting more media of payment in place of income-yielding assets.

readily as marriage licenses. Of course one must pay to get media of payment, even as one must pay for marriage licenses; but in neither case must the payment be made because of the "scarcity" of the thing paid for.

Do people "prefer" liquidity?

To define interest as the "reward for parting with liquidity" is inadmissible also for the simple reason that people do not prefer to hold their wealth in the form of liquid assets. Owners of wealth would indeed be insane if they "preferred," as a general rule, to hold their wealth in the form of media of payment. But they do not. They prefer to hold assets which they hope will yield them income (or capital gains). In fact, the desire for an income from property (or for capital gains) is the chief motive for the accumulation of wealth. People want to hold media of payment in preference to other assets only when they expect that by postponing the purchase of other assets they can get a larger property income, avoid capital losses, or make capital gains.

APOLOGETIC CHARACTER OF LIQUIDITY PREFERENCE THEORY

Like the "abstinence" theory of interest, the "liquidity preference" theory represents interest as a "reward." The propounders of the abstinence theory said interest is a "reward" for abstaining from consumption. Keynes said interest is the "reward" for parting with liquidity. In both theories interest is made to appear as a compensation for sacrifice, for a service rendered to the community. In actual fact interest, like other property incomes, is a reward for nothing other than the ownership of wealth. By owning wealth a person renders a service only to himself. In a society in which the ownership of wealth can be a source of income, it is of course advantageous to own wealth. A person therefore renders himself a service by accumulating wealth and putting it into the form of assets expected to yield the highest return possible. But to say that the income derived from these assets—whether this income takes the form of interest, dividends, rent or profit—is a "reward," is rather perverse. It has an apologetic flavor—it suggests a justification for, instead of an explanation of, interest as property income.

That Keynes couched his interest theory in such disingenuous, apologetic language is puzzling in view of his apparent hostility to "rentiers." Not only did he foresee the "euthanasia of the rentier"; he actually advocated the abolition of interest. (See Chapter XIX, below.)

INTEREST AS PROPERTY INCOME AND AS A PAYMENT FOR A SERVICE

Keynes's suggestion that interest be abolished implies that interest as a property income (the income of the rentier) is not necessary to the proper functioning of the economy. Interest, however, is not merely a property income. Interest has a twofold character: it is a property income and it is also a payment for a service. As a property income interest is not necessary and could be abolished; as a service payment interest is necessary.

As a property income interest may be regarded as a contractual form of profit. This is how the classical economists dealt with interest. J. S. Mill, for instance, though he did devote a separate chapter to interest in his *Principles of Political Economy*, treated interest as one of the constituent parts into which profit could be resolved. Interest could be viewed as that fixed amount of profit which the residual owners of a business firm obligate themselves to pay to those capitalists who had contributed capital to the firm, but who preferred a fixed return on their investment to the more uncertain, though possibly larger, return of the residual owners. Viewed as a form of profit, interest is of course no more a "reward" for anything except the ownership of income-yielding assets than is profit or any other property income.

Viewed as a payment for a service, on the other hand, interest is indeed a "reward" for the rendering of this service. What service is it for which interest is the "reward"? The service rendered by the commercial banks in providing the community with media of payment. Unless the banks are paid for this service, they will not perform it. As long as the payment takes the form, or the name, of interest, interest must be paid. It must be paid, not as a reward for "parting with liquidity," but as a reward for the performance of a service required by the community. The reward must be large enough to cover the costs of rendering this service (i.e., the costs of maintaining the banking establishment), and also to yield a profit to the banks which render the service.

Of course it would be possible to nationalize the banks and have them operate without charge to the clients, as public schools are run without charge to the pupils. In that case interest would disappear. No borrower would be willing to pay interest to anyone if he could get the media of payment he wants, interest-free, from the banks.

Interest as property income of individuals and interest as compensation for the services of banks are really two different things, rather than merely two aspects of the same thing. The fact that we call these two things by the same name—interest— has obscured the essential difference between them and has bedeviled interest theory which has not clearly differentiated these two phenomena. The classical theory of interest was less confused in this respect than modern theories. The classical economists completely neglected interest as a payment for banking services and treated interest exclusively as a payment to owners of capital. Keynes, on the other hand, defined interest as a payment to "rentiers," but then proceeded to show that the rate of interest is determined by the demand for banking services and the supply of banking services (208). If the payment made to banks for the service of supplying media of payment to the community were known by another name than that of the rentiers' income, this mixup would hardly have been possible.

The distinction between interest as a property income and interest as a service income received by financial institutions is recognized in national income accounting. The receipt of interest by financial institutions cannot be treated as rentiers' income in counting up the national income without distorting the national income totals. For this reason adjustments are made which amount in effect to changing the name of interest received by financial institutions from "interest" to "customers' expenditures for services."

HANSEN'S CRITICISM OF
KEYNES'S INTEREST THEORY

Professor Alvin H. Hansen criticized Keynes's interest theory as being "indeterminate." This is the same fault for which Keynes rejected the classical interest theory.[3]

The classical theory said that the interest rate is determined by the interaction of the demand for capital and the supply of capital, i.e., by investment (I) and saving (S), while income (Y) is assumed to remain unchanged. Keynes called this a "nonsense theory," pointing out that for every magnitude of I there must be a different Y, and for every magnitude of Y there is a different S. The classical formulation, said Keynes, can tell us how large Y will be if the rate of interest is at this or that level, provided we have an I function and a whole series (a "family") of S functions, each corresponding to a different level of Y. (See Diagram 11.) But the classical theory cannot tell us what the rate of interest will be, because this depends on which S function will be relevant—and this in turn depends on the level of Y, which depends on the volume of I.

Hansen argued that Keynes's liquidity preference theory is subject to the same criticism. L depends on Y. There should be a separate L function for each level of Y.

A correct theory of interest, said Hansen, can be formulated only by combining the liquidity preference theory with the classical theory. In other words, to say that L and M are the sole determinants of the rate of interest is not any more correct than it is to say that S and I are the sole determinants of the rate of interest.

The complaint that with the Keynesian interest theory "no solution is possible" really rests on the contention that changes in the supply of M cause shifts in the demand for M. (Changes

3. Hansen, A Guide to Keynes, pp. 140 ff.

in the supply of M affect the rate of interest; the rate of interest affects investment; investment affects income; and income affects the demand for M.) The same objection can be raised against all demand-and-supply analysis. Every change in the supply, and consequently in the price, of a commodity brings about changes in Y. A reduction in the price of a commodity means an increase in the real income of the consumer; a rise in price constitutes a corresponding decline in income. These changes in income, in turn, will cause the demand to shift. Here, too, "no solution is possible."

But recognition of this complexity does not require us to reject demand-and-supply analysis. It is still meaningful to say that the price of automobiles is determined by the interaction of the demand for and the supply of automobiles. Similarly, it is still meaningful to say that the rate of interest is a price, determined by demand and supply—and to identify what it is

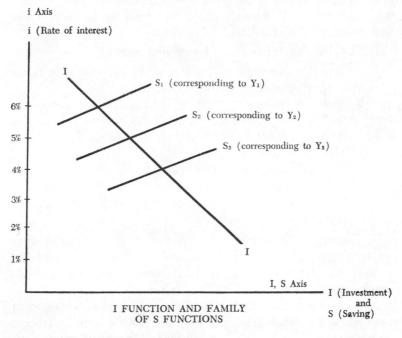

i Axis

i (Rate of interest)

S_1 (corresponding to Y_1)

S_2 (corresponding to Y_2)

S_3 (corresponding to Y_3)

6%

5%

4%

3%

2%

1%

I, S Axis

I (Investment)
and
S (Saving)

I FUNCTION AND FAMILY
OF S FUNCTIONS

Diagram 11

that interest is the price of, and the demand for what and supply of what determine this price. That this price, like all prices, in determined by a multiplicity of factors and that consequently "no solution is possible" is not important. What is important is that Keynes pointed out that interest is the price paid for holding media of payment and that this price is determined primarily by the demand for and the supply of media of payment and not, as was previously believed, by the demand for and supply of capital.

REFORMULATION OF THE THEORY OF INTEREST

What has been said in the present chapter regarding the inconsistencies and contradictions of Keynes's interest theory is sufficient to enable us to reformulate the theory more correctly.

1. Interest is the price paid to obtain media of payment; it is the price which equates the demand for media of payment with the supply of media of payment.

2. The demand for media of payment arises
   a. from the need for such media in carrying out transactions (transactions motive) and
   b. from the desire of people to hold assets that cannot depreciate in terms of the monetary unit when they expect the prices of other assets to decline (speculative motive). This speculative demand for media of payment, it should be noted, arises only when the holding of media of payment is expected to be more advantageous than the holding of other assets; it does not spring from a general preference for liquidity.

3. The supply of media of payment comes from the commercial banks. Providing the community with media of payment is the main function of commercial banks. Commercial banks create media of payment by making loans or by purchasing securities. When they make loans or purchase securities, commercial banks exchange their own debts (in the form of deposits or bank notes) for the debts of individuals, corporations, govern-

ments, and so on; they convert debts with low circulation power into "high-powered" debts. These high-powered debts are what the community uses as media of payment.

In providing the community with media of payment the commercial banks incur costs. These costs, together with a profit, the banks cover by charging and receiving interest.

4. At a given interest rate, the commercial banks tend to supply the community with all the media of payment the community desires. (The supply of media of payment, therefore, is portrayed more correctly by a horizontal than by a vertical line.) Commercial banks behave similarly to other businesses which set a price for their product and then produce as much as they can sell at that price. They do not fix the quantity of their output and then sell it at whatever prices they can get for this quantity.

5. Although interest is the price paid to commercial banks for supplying media of payment, interest is also paid to, and received by, individuals and non-banking firms. Anyone who has media of payment can lend them to others, i.e., can buy interest-bearing debts. There is a sort of secondhand, or secondary, market for media of payment. The rate of interest at which loans are made in this secondary market is the same as the rate charged by commercial banks. Borrowers in the secondary market will always be willing to pay as much as, but no more than, the interest they would have to pay a bank.[4]

Transactions in the secondary market for media of payment do not affect the community's demand for and supply of media of payment. At a given rate of interest the community will want to hold a given amount of media of payment and this amount will be provided by the commercial banks which are the sole creators of media of payment (disregarding, for simplicity, the relatively unimportant amounts of media of payment created

4. This applies only to the types of loans which can be made, and are made, by commercial banks. There are, of course, other types of loans which custom or law do not allow commercial banks to make. In the present discussion, however, it is assumed—as it was assumed by Keynes—that there is only one interest rate. This assumption implies a second assumption: that there is only one type of interest-bearing debt.

by government). If now some people want to increase their holdings of media of payment, while others want to reduce theirs by an equal amount, the community's demand for media of payment is not affected. Those with surplus holdings can lend this surplus to those who want to increase their holdings. The lenders reap the interest which the banks would have received if the borrowers had gone to the banks instead. But if surplus holdings are not equal to requirements for additional holdings of media of payment, this indicates that the community's demand for media of payment in the primary market has changed; and the quantity of media of payment furnished by commercial banks will change correspondingly (assuming the banks have not changed the rate of interest at which they are willing to hold debts).

6. Individuals (and non-bank firms) can receive interest as a property income only because, and as long as, interest must be paid to commercial banks as the price for their services as creators of media of payment. If banks were to make loans interest-free, no one would be able to get an interest income, because no borrower would be willing to pay interest to a non-bank lender if he could obtain an interest-free loan from a bank.

Chapter Seventeen

The Theory of Money and Prices

The title of Keynes's *General Theory of Employment, Interest and Money* leads the reader to expect that the theory of money occupies an important place in his work. This expectation would be further justified by Keynes's previous interests as an economist. He was first and foremost a monetary economist, as is indicated by the names of his earlier books on economics—*Indian Currency and Finance; A Tract on Monetary Reform; A Treatise on Money.* Money and its role in the economy were his chief concern.

Yet the *General Theory* is not really, or at least not primarily, a monetary theory. In the forefront of Keynes's principal work are the theory of employment (as the title indicates), the theory of aggregate demand and supply, investment, consumption, and the relation of these variables to income, output, and employment. The theory of money has been pushed into the background where it plays only a minor role.

THREE MEANINGS OF MONETARY THEORY

To clarify this statement it is necessary to explain what is meant by the "theory of money," or "monetary theory."

Monetary theory can mean three things which, though related, are nevertheless separate and distinct.

1. Monetary theory can mean the theory of the nature of "money," dealing with such questions as: What is money? What is the monetary unit? What is credit? Banking? The theory of money in this sense analyses the various institutions which constitute the monetary system and explains how this system functions. Keynes had paid some attention to these questions in his *Treatise on Money,* but he gave them no consideration in the *General Theory.*

2. Monetary theory can mean the theory of a monetary economy, explaining the behavior of an economy in which people receive money incomes and spend money incomes and can choose to hold "money" (media of payment) in the place of other assets. Since all modern economies are monetary economies, one might think that all economic theory would be "monetary theory" in this sense. Pre-Keynesian economists, however, neglected this feature of the economic system and analyzed economic processes as if they took place on a barter basis. Keynes, on the other hand, stressed the role of "money," thus developing a theory of a monetary economy. His emphasis, however, was chiefly on one particular way in which the existence of money affects economic behavior. "A monetary economy," he wrote, "is essentially one in which changing views about the future are capable of influencing the quantity of employment" (vii). Keynes's "theory of a monetary economy" thus is really a "theory of expectations" rather than a theory of money.[1]

3. Monetary theory can mean the theory which deals with the effects of changes in the quantity of media of payment on prices and production. This is the usual meaning of monetary theory. It is especially monetary theory in this sense which Keynes "pushed back," as he himself expressed it (vi).

EVOLUTION OF KEYNES'S VIEWS REGARDING THE ROLE OF MEDIA OF PAYMENT

In earlier works Keynes had centered his attention on the relation between media of payment and prices. By the time he came to write the *General Theory* he had reached the conclusion that this relationship did not have the significance previously accorded to it. In the first place, Keynes had come to reject the idea that fluctuations in price levels are synonymous with business cycles, as had been implied by many pre-Keynesian economists; he held that, on the contrary, price level fluctuations play only a subsidiary part in cyclical fluctuations and that

1. See Dillard, "The Theory of a Monetary Economy" in Kurihara, *Post-Keynesian Economics*.

primary attention should be given to fluctuations in output and employment. In the second place, Keynes had come to recognize that neither fluctuations in output and employment, nor in price levels, are due primarily to changes in the quantity of media of payment; and that if media of payment have an effect on prices, this effect is much more indirect than was supposed by the "quantity theorists."

The evolution of Keynes's thought on this subject can be traced in the equations which he formulated in successive works and which epitomize the views he held at successive times.

His starting point was the traditional "quantity theory of money." This theory had been formulated in two types of "equations of exchange":

$$P = \frac{MV}{T}, \text{ the "cash transactions" equation, and}$$

$$P = \frac{M}{KT}, \text{ the "cash balances" equation.}$$

The meaning of the first equation is that P, the general price level, is determined by M, the quantity of money (media of payment), multiplied by V, the velocity of turnover of money (the number of times each unit of media of payment is used, on an average, during a given period, say a year) and by T, the volume of transactions requiring the use of media of payment (or "cash"). The greater MV (also called the "effective quantity of money"), the higher, other things remaining equal, will be the price level; the greater T, other things remaining equal, the lower will be the price level, as more business must be transacted with the same amount of media of payment and consequently a smaller amount of such media is available on an average for each unit of goods to be bought and sold.

In the second equation K expresses the ratio of the amount of media of payment held by the people of the community to the total volume of transactions. Thus, if T represents total transactions in one year, and if people held an amount of media of payment equal to one month's transactions requirements, K = 1/12. KT is the amount of "command over goods" which people want to hold in the form of media of payment, (or "cash balances," in the form of cash in pocket and cash in the form of bank balances). Suppose now that people want to increase their cash balances by 20%, so that these will equal 1/10 instead of 1/12 of the year's transactions. What will be the effect on prices? if M is increased by 20% at the same time that people want to increase their cash balances by 20%, prices will remain unchanged. But if M remains unchanged, prices must fall until the unchanged M represents 1/10 instead of 1/12 of the year's total volume of transactions. Contrariwise, if people want to reduce their cash balances (other things, including M, remaining unchanged) prices will rise until the unchanged M represents the smaller amount of "command over goods" which the people wanted to hold in the form of M.

In the first equation the demand for media of payment is T, cash transactions. This equation, accordingly, is called the "cash transactions equation," to differentiate it from the second equation which is known as the "cash balances equation" because in this equation the demand for media of payment, KT, is regarded as a demand for "cash balances." Alfred Marshall was the originator of the "cash balances" approach to monetary theory. Most Cambridge economists, including Keynes, followed his lead. Hence the "cash balances" equation is sometimes referred to as the "Cambridge" equation of exchange.

In *A Tract on Monetary Reform* (1923), Keynes formulated a new equation:

$$p = \frac{n}{k + rk'}$$

The meanings of the symbols are:

$p =$ price level

$n =$ note (and coin) currency

$k =$ amount of "command over goods" people want to hold in the form of cash in pocket.

$k' =$ amount of "command over goods" people want to hold in the form of bank deposits.

$r =$ ratio of cash reserves held by banks to deposits. Thus if banks hold $1 in cash for every $10 in deposits, $r = 1/10$.

This equation calls attention to the two ways in which note currency can be used. Note currency, usually emitted only by the central bank, is used not only by individuals as "cash in pocket" and as "till money" of business firms, but also as reserves held by banks against their deposit obligations.[2]

The equation suggests, therefore, that the price level can be influenced through central bank policy in two ways: 1) by changing the quantity of n emitted by the central bank and 2) by changing r, the reserve ratio. Essentially, however, the "Monetary Reform" equation is only a refinement of $P = \dfrac{M}{KT}$. Keynes wanted to explain the price level and its determinants: these determinants, according to the equation, are the quantity of media of payment supplied by the banks on the one hand; and, on the other hand, the public's demand for "cash balances."

Quite different are the equations which Keynes developed in *A Treatise on Money* (1930). Here he differentiated between the determinants of the general price level and the determinants of partial price levels, especially the price level of investment goods and the price level of consumers' goods. A glance at the consumers' goods price level equation will suffice to show the marked deviation of this type of equation from the previous equations of exchange. The equation is $P = \dfrac{E}{O} + \dfrac{I' - S}{R}$, where

P = price level of consumers' goods

E = earnings of factors of production

O = total output (in real terms)

I' = cost of production of new investments

S = saving (out of factor incomes)

R = volume of consumers' goods purchased by consumers.

The meaning of the equation is that the price level of consumers' goods is determined by two sets of conditions: 1) the

2. This applies more to England and some European countries than to the United States. But, with modifications, the conclusions apply to any economy with a banking system operating on the principle of fractional reserves.

relation of earnings to output; e.g., if wages (and other factor earnings) rise while output remains unchanged, prices will rise; 2) the relation between current saving and current investment expenditures; if $S = I'$, then $I' - S = 0$ and the effect of the saving-investment relation on prices is zero. But if S is not equal to I', then the saving-investment relation will have an effect on prices. If people save more than the amounts currently invested, prices will fall; if they save less than this amount, prices will rise. How much will prices rise or fall? This will depend on how large the difference between S and I' is in relation to the value of consumers' goods purchased.

What is notable about this equation is that all reference to "money" has disappeared from it. Prices are still the "quaesitum" (the thing to be explained) but the quantity of media of payment, the velocity of turnover of media of payment, the demand for cash balances, bank reserve ratios, are no longer regarded as determinants of the price level.

The cleft between Keynes and traditional monetary theory is widened still further in the *General Theory*. The equation $Y = C + I$, which sums up the fundamental idea of this work, contains no reference either to "money" or to the price level.

DETERMINANTS OF THE GENERAL PRICE LEVEL

Although the *General Theory* is primarily concerned with the determinants of income and employment rather than of prices, it nevertheless also deals with the question of what determines the price level.

According to Keynes the general price level is determined

1. by money wages (and other factor remunerations, though Keynes put primary emphasis on wages and in fact regarded labor as the only factor of production), a rise in money wages, other things remaining unchanged, having the effect of raising prices, and

2. by "the scale of output as a whole, i.e., (taking equipment and technique as given) [by] the volume of employment" (294). As employment increases, diminishing returns set in, each

man-hour of work results in less output, and consequently, with given wages, prices must rise.

The relation of the quantity of media of payment to the general price level. The theory of prices.

If these are the determinants of the general price level, then it would seem that the quantity of media of payment has nothing to do with prices. Like individual prices, so the general price level is determined by the relation between the demand for goods and the supply of goods—not, as pre-Keynesian economists (including Keynes himself up to 1930) had contended, by the relation between the supply of media of payment and the demand for media of payment.

Yet in spite of his demonstration that changes in the price level are not (or at least not directly and primarily) brought about by changes in the quantity of media of payment, Keynes paradoxically defined the Theory of Prices as "the analysis of the relation between changes in the quantity of money and changes in the price-level" (296). What, then, is the relation between changes in M—the quantity of money (media of payment)—and changes in the price level?

Changes in M can have an effect on the general price level only via their effects on the demand for goods and the supply of goods.

Effects of changes in M on the supply of goods

For purposes of the analysis in this chapter, the supply of goods must be given a meaning different from the meaning it was given in Chapter II. There aggregate supply was defined as the schedule relating various quantities of output and employment to the *minimum aggregate proceeds* for which firms are willing to sell this output. Here aggregate supply must be understood to mean the schedule relating various quantities of output and employment to the *price level*, i.e., to the average of prices per unit of goods sold.

A change in M could induce firms to raise or lower the prices at which they offer goods only if it affected their per unit costs of production. The only cost of production that could be affected by a change in M is interest cost, because the rate of interest, as we have seen, depends in part on M. But changes in interest rates generally have only an insignificant effect on total production costs, the principal constituent of which is wages. In fact, as pointed out earlier, Keynes assumed that wages were the only cost of production and accordingly disregarded the cost aspect of interest entirely. On Keynes's assumptions, then, changes in M could not affect the supply of goods. The only possible effect of M on prices would be through the aggregate demand for goods.

Effects of changes in M on the demand for goods

False identification of M with Y. Pre-Keynesian economists tended to identify a change in M with a change in Y (income) and then further assumed that changes in Y are synonymous with changes in the effective demand for goods. One of Keynes's most important ideas was that a change in income does not guarantee an equal change in aggregate demand. But the first-mentioned assumption of traditional theory—the assumption that a change in M constitutes a change in Y—is also inadmissible. An increase in M may result, for instance, from a purchase of securities by banks from the public—the former preferring to hold securities, the latter preferring to hold media of payment. There is an exchange of assets, but income is not affected in any way.

To get around this difficulty, some economists concede that it is only when an increase in M accrues to someone as additional income that it could be expected to have any bearing on effective demand. But even this statement is false, because media of payment can never be income by Keynes's definitions. M and Y belong to different categories and cannot be regarded as in any way synonymous or similar. Y, in the sense of *real* income is the stream of goods and services currently produced; or, in the sense of *money* income, it is the payments (or receipts, or proceeds) received by the income recipient. M, on the other hand, consists of the *media* of payment with which these payments are made and with the aid of which the community distributes the income and exchanges the goods currently produced. Income (Y) may be thought of as a *stream of goods*; the media of payment (M) as the buckets used by people to dip into the stream and to secure the particular goods they want. Or, if income is thought of as *payments*, media of payment are —just that: the media for making the payments. Under no circumstances can media of payment be real income or money income. To identify real income or money income with media of payment is like identifying food or eating with eating implements. Just as additional spoons do not constitute additional eating or additional food, so additional M does not constitute additional money income or additional real income.[3]

Relation of M to investment. How, then, can changes in M affect the effective demand for goods? Only through their effect on the rate of interest and, through the rate of interest, on investment. An increase in M will tend to lower i (rate of interest). By how much it will lower it depends, of course, on the liquidity preference schedule (L), i.e., on the demand for M. As was shown in Chapter XV, this demand is generally inelastic at relatively high values of i, but is highly elastic at low values of i. In other words, if i is, say, 6%, a relatively small increase in M may lower i to 4%, but if i were 3% to start with, the same increase in M might reduce i to only 2½%. At about 2%, Keynes said, the demand for M is probably perfectly elastic, so that no matter how much M may be increased, i would not fall below 2%. (See Diagram 10.) A given increase in M, then, may or may not effectively reduce i, depending on the elasticity of the L function.

The next question is: how effectively does a decrease in i stimulate investment, or an increase in i discourage it? The answer is that the interest elasticity of investment is low. Investment does not so readily respond to changes in i as it does

3. The analogy of the eating implements may seem farfetched, but has an historical basis. An ancient Greek coin, the *obolus* (a spit, a pointed pillar; cf. obelisk), was originally a small spear handed out to participants in temple feasts and entitling the holder to a piece of meat. Later this sacred eating implement became a token of general purchasing power, entitling the holder to any commodity of a value equal to what originally had been the value of the meat.

to changes in r (the marginal efficiency of capital), i.e., to changes in profit expectations.

Relation of changes in I to changes in effective demand. The next link in the chain transmitting the effects of a change in M to the price level is the effect which a change in investment has on effective demand. This is the now familiar multiplier effect. In a community in which people consume a large proportion of any additional income they receive, the multiplier will be large. A change in I will produce much larger changes in consumption. Effective demand will increase by a large multiple of any increase in investment. If the multiplier is low, a given change in I will have a correspondingly small effect on effective demand. But whether the multiplier is high or low, a change in M will not change effective demand unless the change in M affects i, and i affects I.

Relation of changes in effective demand to changes in price level. The shape of the supply function. Assuming that investment, and consequently effective demand, do actually increase as a result of the decline in i brought about by an increase in M, what would be the effect of this increase in effective demand on prices? To answer this question it is necessary to look at supply. What is the shape of the supply function (here defined as the schedule relating various quantities of output and employment to the price level) and at which point of this function does the economy find itself?

As long as there are unemployed workers and other unemployed resources available, firms are generally willing and able to meet an increase in the demand for goods by producing more goods without raising prices. Assuming that this is so, supply would be perfectly elastic as long as there is any unemployment. When full employment has been reached, however, supply is totally inelastic. Output cannot be expanded any more, and any increase in demand must result in higher prices. This is illustrated in Diagram 12A.

The horizontal axis measures output in numbers of people employed; the vertical axis measures the price level. The S — S line is the supply function, showing the output which firms are willing to produce at various price levels; if the price level is at

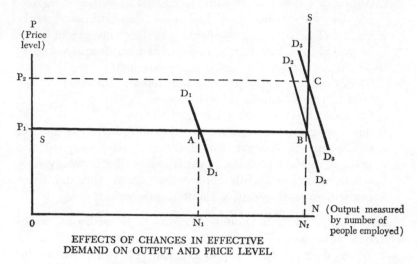

EFFECTS OF CHANGES IN EFFECTIVE
DEMAND ON OUTPUT AND PRICE LEVEL

Diagram 12 A

P_1, firms are ready to produce any output from zero to N_t (full employment output), depending on the size of the demand. Supply is perfectly elastic from O to N_t. At N_t supply becomes inelastic. Regardless of how much the demand for goods may rise, the quantity of goods produced cannot be larger than full employment output N_t. If demand is D_1, intersecting the supply function at A, the quantity of output will be ON_1 and the price level will be P_1. If demand increases to D_2, intersecting the supply function at B, output will rise to ON_t while the price level remains unchanged at P_1. But if demand rises to D_3, intersecting the supply function at C, output remains unchanged at N_t, while the price level rises to P_2.

The shape of the supply function shown in Diagram 12A is not, however, a true representation of supply conditions. It would be unrealistic to assume the supply function to be perfectly price-elastic up to the point of full employment and to become suddenly perfectly inelastic at that point. Even before full employment has been reached an increase in demand will force prices up for the following reasons:

1. Although wages may remain unchanged as output increases, physical productivity may decline because additional workers are less skilled or because obsolete equipment must be pulled back into use, or because of more frequent breakdowns, as productive facilities are strained.

2. Money wages may actually not remain unchanged, but tend to rise as employment increases.

3. Compensations of other factors increase.

4. Since supply conditions are not the same for all industries, the supply of some commodities will have reached the point of perfect inelasticity even before the economy as a whole has achieved full employment, while other industries can still expand output without raising prices.

The supply function should accordingly be redrawn, as in Diagram 12B. According to this revised supply function an increase in demand from D_1 to D_2 will still call forth an increase in output, but only from ON_1 to ON_2, while the price level will rise from P_1 to P_2. The relative increase in output, however, is still greater than the relative rise in the price level.

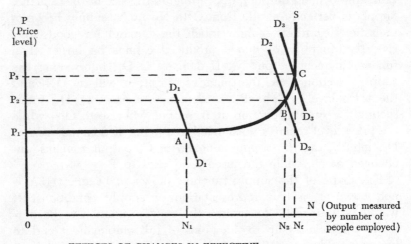

EFFECTS OF CHANGES IN EFFECTIVE
DEMAND ON OUTPUT AND PRICE LEVEL

Diagram 12 B

A further increase in demand to D_3, on the other hand, will lead chiefly to a rise in the price level, to P_3, and only to a relatively small increase in output to N_f. Any further increase in demand could not call forth additional output and would only raise the price level.

SUMMARY

Keynes argued that changes in M could affect the price level only through their effects on the aggregate demand for goods and the aggregate supply of goods. Such effects are possible only through the changes in i (interest rate) which may be called forth by changes in M. Changes in i may cause changes in investment and hence in effective demand, i.e., in total expenditures.

Changes in effective demand will call forth changes in output and employment. At low levels of output and employment, firms are generally willing to meet increases in demand by producing more without raising prices. When levels of output and employment are already high, further expansion of output is generally associated with price increases because industry runs into diminishing returns and money wages are likely to rise.

To recapitulate, the effects of changes in M on the price level will depend on

1. The effect of a change in M on i. Generally, a change in M will affect i significantly when i is relatively high, but not when i is low.
2. The effect of i on I. Empirical studies of the responsiveness of investment decisions to changes in i have borne out Keynes's opinion that i has little effect on I. It is r (the marginal efficiency of capital, or profit expectations) rather than i which importantly influences I.
3. The effect of I on effective demand. A given change in I will have a larger or smaller effect on effective demand (i.e., total expenditures) depending on the multiplier, which in turn depends on the marginal consumption ratio The multiplier tends to be high in underdeveloped countries,

but low in advanced industrial countries. When the multiplier is low, a given change in I will not greatly change
effective demand.

4. The effect of a change in effective demand on the price
level. A change in effective demand will not affect the
price level significantly if output is well below the full
employment level. In this case output rather than prices
will change in response to changes in total expenditures.
The closer the economy is to full employment, the more
will changes in aggregate demand be met by price changes
rather than by changes in output.

In each of these four links connecting a change in M with a
change in the price level, some or all of the effects of the change
in M may be lost. As a result, the net effect of changes in M
on prices is generally small. Keynes argued, in substance, that
changes in the price level were due, not to changes in M, but
to changes in wages; or, conversely, that stability of the price
level (or of the "value of money," which is reflected in the
price level) can not be achieved by regulating M, as pre-
Keynesian economists taught, but that it depends on the stability
of wages.

Chapter Eighteen

The Keynesian "Revolution"

In Chapter I, reference was made to the "revolutionary" character of Keynes's theory, and to Keynes's own opinion, expressed in a letter to G. B. Shaw, that his theory would "revolutionize" economic thinking. In several places in the preceding chapters attention has been called to the contrast between Keynesian and traditional economic doctrine. The present chapter summarizes the "revolutionary" features of Keynesian economics.

1. *The problem is to explain the volume of employment.* The question Keynes set out to answer and around which he built his theory was: what determines the volume of employment, output and income? This was a departure from the traditional theory which asked: what determines the prices of commodities and the distribution of income? From the days of Ricardo to the days of Keynes the "orthodox" or "classical" economic theory was primarily a theory of value and distribution; it rested on the assumption that the volume of employed resources at any time was given. The problem of economics as the classical economists saw it was to explain the allocation of these employed resources to different uses and the distribution of the product among those who had contributed to its production.

To put it differently: the traditional economics assumed "full" employment; Keynes explained why full employment is a rare "special case" and why usually a greater or lesser degree of unemployment prevails. Traditional economic theory is a special theory, valid only for the special case of full employment, whereas Keynes's *general* theory is valid for all levels of employment.

2. *Repudiation of Say's law.* A corollary of the traditional assumption of full employment was the acceptance of Say's law. This law states that aggregate demand is always equal to aggregate supply; that as more goods are produced, people also demand more goods, since the only reason why they produce more is that they want to acquire the means either to consume more or to accumulate capital goods; that consequently aggregate demand could never be insufficient to absorb any output, no matter how large.

Keynes disproved Say's law. He was not the first to have attacked it, but previous challengers had not convinced their fellow economists, while Keynes's refutation of Say's law was conclusive. He argued that as output rises, consumption rises too, but not by so much as output. The increasing gap between total output and the portion of it which is consumed must be filled by investment, i.e., by additions to capital. Intended investment, however, may not be large enough to fill this gap at high levels of income, though it may be larger than the gap at low levels of income; consequently output—and income—must adjust themselves to a level at which the gap between total output and the part of output that is consumed will be just equal to the amount of intended investment.

Stated differently: traditional economics regarded the volume of current investment as determined by current saving. It said that if people saved more out of a given income, the result would be a corresponding increase in investment. Keynes showed that saving does not lead to investment, but merely to a diminution of income.

3. *Wage cuts cannot stimulate employment.* Another corollary of the traditional assumption of full employment was the proposition that all those who want to work are always assured of finding jobs, provided they are willing to accept a sufficiently low (real) wage—one which would not exceed their contribution to output. Keynes denied this. He argued that a general lowering of wages would not lead to greater employment and output, because as wages fall, income falls, and as income falls, aggregate demand for goods falls, and it is aggregate demand which determines the level of employment.

The idea that, in a depression, unemployed workers could all find jobs if only they lowered their wage demands is wrong, said Keynes. Not a reduction in wages, but an increase in aggregate demand, is the remedy for unemployment.

4. *Attention shifted from supply to demand.* Traditional theory, assuming that aggregate demand was created automatically by aggregate supply, devoted its attention to the analysis of supply. Keynes, accepting the traditional theory of supply, centered attention on demand; he showed that effective demand is not automatically sufficient to absorb all quantities of output; that it is, in fact, the chronic insufficiency of effective demand which is at the root of our economic difficulties.

5. *Attention shifted from micro-economics to macro-economics.* Pre-Keynesian economists had given primary attention to the behavior of the small economic units—the individual, the firm, the industry. Keynes centered his attention on economic aggregates, such as aggregate output, aggregate demand, aggregate employment. Whereas traditional economics was primarily "micro-economics" (from the Greek *mikron*—small), Keynes shifted attention to "macro-economics" (from the Greek *makron* —big).

Keynes pointed out that many conclusions derived from micro-economics do not apply to the behavior of the economy viewed as a whole, as had been believed by the classical economists. Adam Smith had said that "what is prudence in the conduct of every private family can scarce be folly in that of a great Kingdom,"[1] and his followers down to Keynes were inclined to regard this as self-evident. If any individual can get richer by consuming less and saving more, so they reasoned, the community as a whole, too, will get richer by consuming less. Again, if any firm can expand its output and employ more people by cutting wages, then general wage cuts throughout the community must increase aggregate employment.

Keynes showed that a community does not get richer by consuming less, but that on the contrary, it gets poorer as a result; that a decrease in consumption leads to curtailment of produc-

1. Smith, *Wealth of Nations*, Everyman's Library Edition, I, 401.

tion and to unemployment. Any individual can get richer by consuming less and saving more, but only on the assumption (which was not specifically stated by micro-economists) that the community as a whole would *not* reduce its consumption. The argument that wage cuts will increase the number of people employed is based on a similar tacit assumption. Any firm can expand its output and employ more people at lower wages, but only on the assumption (not specifically stated by micro-economists) that there are no over-all wage cuts throughout the economy. If wages were cut all around, the effect would be not only to reduce production costs, but also to reduce income and thus to lessen the aggregate demand for goods; the more the firms cut costs in an effort to expand their sales, the more do they saw away the props from under their market. Wage cuts are helpful to any individual firm, but useless to the economy as a whole.

These mistaken applications to the whole economy of conclusions which are valid for any of its parts are examples of the "fallacy of composition."

6. *Integration of value theory with monetary theory.* Not all pre-Keynesian economists, however, can be classified as micro-economists. Traditional economic theory may be regarded as having been composed of two separate branches: value theory and monetary theory. Value theory—the main body of pre-Keynesian economics—was micro-economics. Only monetary theory dealt with macro-economic concepts: the price level and the quantity of media of payment. Value theory explained how prices of commodities and of factors of production are formed by the interaction of demand and supply. But this theory was built on the assumption of full employment and of a stable price level, i.e., an unchanging "value of money." Monetary theory, on the other hand, explained fluctuations in price levels (i.e., changes in the "value of money"), and the economic disturbances associated with such fluctuations.

Keynes rejected the traditional view "of regarding the influence of money as something so to speak separate from the general theory of supply and demand" (vi). In his reformulation of economics, monetary theory was merged with demand-and-supply theory to explain fluctuations of output and employment and, less importantly, of the general price level. Keynes showed that the theory of demand and supply, extended to include *aggregate* demand and *aggregate* supply, is quite capable of explaining fluctuations in output, employment, and prices, which had previously been attributed to the disturbing effects of "money." But of course it can do so only if freed from the assumption that full employment and a stable price level always prevail.

The integration of two previously separate theories—the theory dealing with prices and output of individual commodities and the theory dealing with price level fluctuations—into one general theory of employment, output, and "money" is a second reason why Keynes called his theory a *general* theory.

7. *The amount of saving depends on the amount of investment.* The relationship between investment and saving was shown by Keynes to be the reverse of what traditional economics said it was. According to the old theory, investment depends on the willingness of people to save; the more people save, the more can be, and will be, invested. The only reason why more capital is not accumulated is that people are not thrifty enough.

Keynes argued that investment does not depend on the community's thriftiness, but on profit expectations. The amount of actual saving, however, depends on how much is being invested. If nothing is invested, the entire income is consumed and nothing is saved. If investments are being made, i.e., if the community's capital is being enlarged, the portion of income devoted to this enlargement cannot have been consumed and must therefore be saved. No matter how much or how little the community *wants* to save, the amount it actually does save is always determined by the amount of current investment.

This apparently paradoxical relationship between saving and investment is epitomized in the so-called *paradox of thrift*: the more the community as a whole wants to save, the less will it actually save. Why? Because a desire to save more out of a given income is the same thing as a decline in expenditures for consumers' goods; this decline weakens the inducement to invest; and if less is invested the amount saved must be correspondingly less. On the other hand, if people want to save less, they consume more; increased consumption encourages investment; and as more is invested, more is saved.

8. *Enterprise, not thrift, is a civic virtue.* A corollary of this revised view of the relation between saving and investment is that thrift can no longer be revered as a civic virtue. The classical economists taught that thrift made nations rich. Keynes showed that thrift never increases wealth, but often impoverishes a nation by plunging it into depression and unemployment. It is through investment that wealth is increased. The people to be hailed as public benefactors are the *entrepreneurs,* not the *rentiers;* the business managers who enlarge the production capacity of the community, not the savers who merely accumulate securities and collect interest.

9. *Public spending justified as a depression remedy.* Another corollary of the new theory of saving and investment is the recognition that a nation can lift itself out of an economic depression through government spending. This was regarded as heresy by most pre-Keynesian economists, as equivalent to "lifting oneself up by one's own bootstraps." The remedy for depression, prescribed by classical economists, was to save more and thus to encourage private investment. Government spending would *dis*courage private investment, they thought, because, in order to spend, the government would either have to increase taxes, which would burden the private economy, or it would have to borrow the "funds" which would otherwise have found their way into private investment.

Keynes showed that government spending during depression, so far from further depressing the economy, would increase consumer expenditures by a multiple of the amount spent by government, and that private investment would be stimulated by this increase in the aggregate demand for goods. The Keynesian *multiplier* theory provided a convincing justification of the previously derided pump-priming schemes for government spending.

10. *Interest is a phenomenon of liquidity preference.* Keynes disproved the classical theory of interest and put a new theory in place of the old. According to the classical view, interest is

the price paid for the use of capital; it equates the demand for capital with the supply of capital—investment with saving. If people save more, the rate of interest must decline until it is low enough to encourage investors to absorb all the current saving of the community; if demand for new capital increases, the rate of interest, other things remaining unchanged, must rise in order to induce people to save the larger amounts required for investment.

Keynes argued that interest is the price paid for the use of media of payment, not for the use of capital; that it equates the demand for media of payment with the supply of media of payment, not the demand for capital with the supply of capital. Interest is not something that must be paid to induce people to *save*, but to induce them to lend out their media of payment. Interest must be paid in order to overcome the *liquidity preference* of people, i.e., their preference for liquid wealth in the form of media of payment; interest is not paid, as the classical economists asserted, to overcome the *time preference* of people, i.e., their preference for consuming now rather than later.

Keynes agreed with the classical economists in saying that saving and investment always tend toward an equilibrium (and of course must always be equal, whether they are in equilibrium or not). But according to Keynes this equilibrium is brought about through fluctuations in income, not though fluctuations in the rate of interest. If the community wants to save more out of a given income while the volume of current investment continues unchanged, income will decline to the level at which the community wants to save no more than the amount currently invested. If investment increases while the people's propensity to save remains unchanged, income will rise to the level at which people want to save the larger amount required.[2]

11. *Money as a store of value.* The role of "money" (i.e., media of payment), in the view of the classical economists, was primarily that of a medium of exchange; Keynes stressed its significance as a store of value. People want media of payment not only because they need a medium of exchange to carry out

2. See points 2 and 9 in this chapter.

business transactions, but because they want to hold wealth in liquid form. They want to hold wealth in this liquid form because the future values of other assets (forms of wealth) are uncertain; if asset values should fall, it would be an advantage to have media of payment with which to buy assets at these lower values.

To the extent that media of payment are held as a form of wealth, they are of course not used to buy goods; therefore, more media of payment do not mean more demand for goods. The increase in the quantity of media of payment may go into "hoards." This is another departure from the traditional theory of money. The classical theory equated media of payment with demand for goods; it assumed that since all "money" is used as a medium of exchange, any additions to its quantity would automatically also increase the demand for goods and thus raise prices. Keynes showed that changes in the quantity of media of payment have no direct effect on demand for goods and on prices. Other things remaining equal, such changes could only affect the rate of interest, and this, in turn, might affect the volume of investment. The effects of changes in the quantity of media of payment on prices are remote and in most cases negligible. The price level, according to Keynes, is determined chiefly by wages and other costs, not by the quantity of media of payment.

12. *The role of expectations.* Finally, Keynes stressed the role of expectations, especially in decisions to invest. Pre-Keynesian economists tended to disregard expectations, emphasizing rather past and present yields of capital equipment as determining the demand for capital. Keynes rejected this view. He regarded it as one of the essential features of a monetary economy that it allows changing views about the future to influence the volume of investment and therefore also the quantity of employment and output.

Chapter Nineteen

Economic Policies Suggested by Keynes

Keynes considered a lively concern with policy to be a virtue in an economist. Scientific detachment and neutrality were not his ideals. Like Adam Smith, he regarded economics "as a branch of the science of a statesman or legislator." His theories were designed to support the economic policies he championed, to win adherents for the course of action he favored.

Keynes recommended policies for the long run as well as for the short run. His prescriptions were for reforms as well as for remedies.

LONG-RUN POLICIES

Basic weaknesses of capitalism

In formulating his policy recommendations, Keynes had in mind the industrially advanced capitalistic countries, not the "underdeveloped" countries which have claimed so much of the attention of economists since the end of World War II. The problems of underdeveloped countries are quite different from those of developed countries; and the policies called for are correspondingly different. In general Keynesian policies are not applicable to underdeveloped countries.

As Keynes saw it, capitalistic countries with highly developed industry, such as Great Britain and the United States, suffer from two chronic diseases:

1. *Instability,* manifested by business cycles and the alternating dangers of inflation and economic contraction.
2. *Unemployment,* due to a deficiency of effective demand.

Economic reforms advocated by Keynes

To free capitalism from its chronic instability and unemployment due to the deficiency of effective demand, Keynes proposed three reforms, aimed at raising and stabilizing aggregate demand:

1. *Redistribution of income.* Taking away from the rich and giving to the poor tends to raise the consumption function. Losing one dollar of income will not cause the rich to curtail their consumption expenditures by as much as the poor will increase theirs when they get an additional dollar of income. Keynes did not argue in favor of complete equality of income, but regarded the inequalities existing in his time as excessive.

Redistribution of income could be achieved through sharply progressive income taxes and death taxes, such as existed in England even before World War II and were introduced in the United States in the 1940's. Progressive taxes reduce the disposable income (incomes left after payment of taxes) of the rich more than those of the poor and consequently reduce the inequality of disposable incomes of persons.

Another recent development tending to raise the propensity to consume and the consumption function, though not stressed by Keynes, is "social security." When people know that in case of unemployment they will get unemployment benefits, and in old age a pension, they do not feel under pressure to save for these contingencies, and are correspondingly inclined to spend a larger portion of their current income on consumption.

2. *Abolition of interest.* Investment is encouraged by a low rate of interest, not by a high rate, as was generally believed before Keynes. Interest is an obstacle to investment. It is only because interest is paid that capital cannot be accumulated to the point at which we have all the capital we can use. To encourage the accumulation of capital, interest must be continually lowered until the rate of interest falls to zero. No one would then any longer be able to get an income from owning debts (e.g., bonds). This "would mean the euthanasia of the rentier [owner of income-yielding securities or other income-yielding property who merely collects the income without taking part

in the management of the income-yielding property], and consequently the euthanasia of the cumulative oppressive power of the capitalist to exploit the scarcity-value of capital" (376).

3. *Socialization of investment.* Because instability and unemployment are due mainly to the volatility of investment, the state should direct investment with a view to assuring continuously full employment. Keynes urged that the state should determine the volume of investment expenditures.

Keynes's reforms aimed at saving capitalism

In advocating the reforms listed in the preceding section, Keynes did not intend to destory capitalism, but on the contrary to save it. He was aware that his reforms "would seem to a nineteenth-century publicist or to a contemporary American financier to be a terrific encroachment on individualism," but he defended them "as the only practicable means of avoiding the destruction of existing economic forms in their entirety and as the condition of the successful functioning of individual initiative" (380).

Keynes did not want to do away with "capitalists," but with "rentiers." The existence of rentiers, he said, marks a passing phase of capitalism. They were necessary only as long as saving had to be encouraged. Now we must encourage spending, not saving. The rentier, therefore, no longer performs a socially useful function. Elimination of the rentier, the "functionless investor," would not impair, but on the contrary would improve, the functioning of the capitalistic economy. The capitalist enterpriser, the active capitalist, would be freed from bondage to the capitalist rentier, the passive capitalist.

In urging that the state assume responsibility for investment Keynes was at pains to point out that he was not advocating the socialization of the instruments of production; he only wanted the state to decide what quantities of production instruments were to be produced. This reform, too, Keynes argued, would improve, rather than interfere with, the functioning of the capitalistic economy. It would ensure that the economy would always operate at full capacity. Like the abolition of interest and the redistribution of income, the socialization of investment "can be introduced gradually and without a break in the general traditions of society" (378).

Contradictions in Keynes's reform proposals

a) Encouraging consumption vs. encouraging investment.

Keynes's reform proposals are consistent in that they all aim at increasing and stabilizing aggregate demand, but there are fundamental conflicts between measures to encourage consumption and measures to encourage investment. Professor Kurihara pointed out that "Keynes's theory of consumption tends to encourage radical policies, while his theory of investment tends to encourage conservative policies."[1] To increase the consumption function calls for income equalization, social security, high income and death taxes, high wages and low profits. All this savors of "radicalism." It is the opposite of what businessmen regard as the conditions favorable to investment. Investment would be stimulated by low taxes, low wages, and high profits and by all measures regarded as "conservative." Depending on whether the former or the latter type of measures is held in view, Keynes appears as a "radical" or as a "conservative." It is worth noting that he was, in fact, claimed as a prophet by socialists as well as by fascists.

b) Euthanasia of rentier or socialization of commercial banks?

Keynes's proposal to eliminate the "functionless investor" is confused through Keynes's failure to distinguish between the two aspects of interest: as a price paid to commercial banks for creating media of payment and as a property income. (See Chapter XVI.) The disappearance of interest would not mean the euthanasia of the rentier, of the functionless investor. The functionless investor would merely hold other assets, (e.g., stocks) instead of holding debts (bonds). What the disappearance of interest would mean is that commercial banks would get no "reward" for their service of creating media of payment. Since the services of commercial banks are indispensable to

1. Kurihara, "Professor Hansen on America's Economic Revolution," *The Economic Journal*, September 1958, p. 481.

the community, the abolition of interest would require either a) that the banks impose their charge under another name, in which case the disappearance of interest would not be real, but only nominal; or b) that the banks be socialized, their lending services offered gratis, and their costs covered out of general taxes.

A proposal to abolish interest is not the same as a proposal to abolish the functionless investor. If Keynes meant to abolish interest in order to free firms of a cost he should have advocated the nationalization, or socialization, of the commercial banks. If he meant to abolish the "functionless investor" class, he should have advocated a 100% tax on all income from property, or the nationalization or socialization of all income-yielding property.

SHORT-RUN POLICIES

Although Keynes did formulate suggestions for long-run policies to overcome the chronic ailments of capitalism—instability and unemployment—his chief concern was with the short run. When depression and unemployment strike, the problem is what to do about it immediately, not how to reform society so as to prevent future recurrence of these evils.

Policies must be geared to changing economic conditions

Policies to be followed in the short run should depend on the economic condition in which a country finds itself at the moment. Different measures are called for when the country is in depression and suffering from unemployment than when it is prosperous, producing at full capacity, and hence in danger of inflation. Keynes has been accused of inconsistency because, at various times, he advocated contradictory policies. For instance, he opposed exchange rate stability in the 1920's and favored it at the Bretton Woods Conference in 1944. But this was not because he was inconsistent. He opposed exchange rate stability for a country suffering from depression unemployment; he favored exchange rate stability in a world of full employment, such as was envisioned at the Bretton Woods Conference. Other seeming contradictions in Keynes's policy recommendations can be explained in the same way. Of course in some cases Keynes repudiated an earlier recommendation simply because he had changed his mind. Thus he partly abandoned his early faith in monetary manipulation as a cure-all, and urged greater reliance on government spending as a depression measure.

Depression policies

Since depressions are due to a deficiency of effective demand, the way to get out of depression is to increase effective demand, i.e., expenditures for consumption and investment.

In the short run little can be done to raise the consumption function. It would be possible to increase consumption somewhat by reducing taxes on the lower and middle income groups, but the effects would be small and long delayed.

What can be done to increase investment expenditures? Investment expenditures depend on the marginal efficiency of capital and the rate of interest. The marginal efficiency of capital, in turn, depends largely on the state of mind of businessmen and for this reason is not readily susceptible to manipulation by public policy; not much can be done to increase the marginal efficiency of capital except to provide a favorable psychological climate.

a) Monetary policy

The second determinant of investment—the rate of interest—can easily be manipulated. To encourage investment, the interest rate should be low. The way to keep the interest rate low is to have the central bank follow an "easy money" policy. The central bank can do this by lending freely at a low rate of interest and by purchasing securities, thereby pouring media of payment into the "money market" and driving the prices of securities (e.g., bonds) up. A rise in the prices of securities means that the interest rate falls.

Although more will be invested at a low than at a high interest rate (other things being equal), the increase in investment due to a lowering of the rate of interest will be small, since investment is relatively inelastic with respect to the rate of interest. Moreover, in a depression the marginal efficiency of capital may be less than zero (because businessmen expect that additional productive equipment would add nothing to their profits and would only cause them losses), so that no matter how low the rate of interest may fall, it will not be low enough to encourage investment.

For these reasons Keynes regarded monetary policy as insufficient to restore a depressed economy to full employment prosperity. The most effective way to overcome a depression is through government intervention.

b) Fiscal policy

Government can intervene in a depression to restore full employment through fiscal policy, i.e., measures pertaining to government revenues and, especially, government expenditures. When consumers' expenditures and investment expenditures are insufficient to induce firms to produce at the full employment level, government expenditures must make up the deficiency of expenditures in the so-called "private sector" of the economy if full employment is to be attained.

Government expenditures may be covered by additional tax revenues or they may be "deficit expenditures," i.e., expenditures in excess of revenues. If the government obtains the media of payment needed for additional expenditures by imposing additional taxes, the tax payments will reduce the income available to the private sector, and consequently consumption expenditures will also be reduced. The extent to which consumption expenditures will be reduced will depend on who pays the additional taxes; taxes imposed on the rich will of course not reduce consumption expenditures as much as taxes imposed on the poor. But if the additional government spending is "deficit spending," no reduction whatever in private spending will result.

The government obtains the media of payment needed for deficit spending by borrowing from the public or by borrowing from the commercial banks, i.e., by selling government securities either to the so-called "non-bank public" (including financial institutions other than commercial banks) or to the commercial banks. In the latter case the quantity of media of payment is increased (because the commercial banks pay for the securities by creating demand deposits for the government); in the former it is not. Consequently, borrowing from the (non-bank) public tends to raise the rate of interest, borrowing from the banks tends to lower it. To get the fullest effect of deficit spending as a recovery measure, the deficits should therefore be financed by borrowing from the commercial banks, since in this way the interest rate can be lowered and investment encouraged. Of course the government could also finance its deficits by issuing paper currency or non-interest bearing securities. The effect of this would be the same as the effect of borrowing from the commercial banks, except that the government would have to pay no interest.

c) "Pump-priming" versus "compensatory fiscal policy"

Government deficit spending has the same effect upon income, output, and employment as have private investment expenditures. A given amount of deficit spending will increase income by a multiple of this amount, depending on the magnitude of the multiplier (i.e., on the community's marginal consumption ratio, which is reflected in the multiplier). The concept of the multiplier provided theoretical support for the "pump-priming" policy much advocated and debated in the depression of the 1930's. The pump-priming idea was that a little government spending would stimulate a flow of private spending, even as a little water poured down the pump will start up a steady flow of water. But the multiplier theory also showed the limitations of the pump-priming idea. A small deficit is not necessarily sufficient to raise income to the full employment level unless the multiplier is very large; and government spending is needed not only to prime the pump of private spending, but to compensate continuously for a chronic deficiency of private spending. The Keynesian analysis therefore does not suggest a "pump-priming" policy so much as it suggests a "compensatory fiscal policy."

Of all the policies advocated by Keynes, fiscal policy as a means to overcome the malfunctioning of the private capitalistic economy is most closely linked to his name. As Adam Smith was the famous champion of *laissez faire*, Karl Marx of socialism,

Friedrich List of protection of infant industries, Henry George of a single tax on land, so Keynes is known as the apostle of deficit spending as a means to recovery from depression.

Anti-inflation policy

Though Keynes was chiefly concerned with how to get a country out of depression and how to keep it from falling into depression, his analysis and policies can also be used to combat or prevent inflation.

Inflation occurs when aggregate expenditures exceed the amount which would call forth a full-employment output at pre-inflation prices. If full employment could be attained with aggregate expenditures of, say $500 billion, then aggregate expenditures of $550 billion would be inflationary, since the extra $50 billion expenditures could not increase output and could lead only to a rise in prices. The extra $50 billion constitutes the "inflationary gap" between expenditures and the value of full-employment output at pre-inflation prices.

To prevent inflation from occurring, the inflationary gap must be closed. In the short run—and this analysis applies only to the short run—it cannot be closed by increasing the labor force or by raising its productivity. It is necessary therefore to reduce expenditures. This can be done in part by a "tight money" policy of high interest rates which will supposedly discourage investment expenditures. But since investment is interest-inelastic, this is not likely to be effective except in case of extreme increases in interest rates. As in the struggle to overcome depression, so also in the fight against inflation fiscal policy must be the principal weapon. Government must spend less than it takes in.

If, as in war, government spending must be increased regardless of inflationary pressures, then the inflationary gap must be closed by cutting down private spending through more drastic measures. Such measures were adopted by all belligerent countries, including the United States, during World War II. Private investment not related to the war effort was forbidden. Also forbidden was the production of passenger automobiles, washing machines, and other durable consumer goods. This necessarily put severe restrictions on consumption. Consumer spending was further reduced through high income taxes, saving drives (virtually amounting, in some instances, to compulsory saving), price control and rationing.

CONTRASTS BETWEEN KEYNESIAN AND PRE-KEYNESIAN POLICIES

The contrasts between Keynesian and pre-Keynesian policies have already been noted in various parts of this book. The tabulation below summarizes these contrasts:

Pre-Keynesian *Keynesian*

1. In depression

Pre-Keynesian	Keynesian
a. increase saving	a. increase spending
b. reduce debts	b. increase debts
c. reduce government expeditures	c. increase government expenditures
d. balance budget	d. unbalance budget
e. reduce wages	e. raise prices; do not reduce wages; even a "once-for-all" wage cut will hinder, rather than promote, recovery

2. In prosperity

Pre-Keynesian	Keynesian
Choke off the boom in time so the inevitable depression following it will not be so severe.	Keep boom going. Depression is not the inevitable consequence of the boom. To choke off a boom in order to soften depression is like killing a healthy man in order to keep him from getting sick.

3. To prevent inflation

Pre-Keynesian	Keynesian
Control the quantity of media of payment.	Control aggregate expenditures.

INTERNATIONAL ECONOMIC POLICIES

In a world plagued by instability and unemployment Keynes favored a policy of economic nationalism, of insulation from economic disturbance emanating from other countries. This involves a) abandonment of international exchange rate stability and b) abandonment of free trade between nations.

International exchange rate stability

Under the international gold standard the principal objective of monetary policy was to preserve the stability of the "external value of money," (i.e., the amount of foreign media of payment that can be had in exchange for one unit of domestic media of payment). This was done by maintaining convertibility of the nation's media of payment into gold and, through gold, into foreign media of payment at fixed rates of exchange. Under this system any recession in one country promptly spread to all others. The first international effect of a recession (i.e., economic contraction) in one country—country A—was a decline in imports by country A from country B and others. Country B's balance of payments was adversely affected and its exchange rate weakened. To defend the "external value" of its "money," country B had to raise its rate of interest. This action was calculated to increase foreign demand for country B's media of payment and to drive domestic prices down to a level at which exports would be increased again. But higher interest rates and lower prices meant recession in country B. Country B would now in turn transmit its recession to other countries by curtailing its purchases from them.

Keynes argued that the policy of maintaining external, or exchange rate, stability should be abandoned in favor of a policy of maintaining internal stability. Rather than jeopardizing prosperity by raising interest rates, Keynes would allow the value of the country's monetary unit to decline in terms of the monetary units of other countries. In this way a country could defend itself against depressive influences from abroad.

A regime of fixed exchange rates is desirable only when continued full employment is assured everywhere. This thought is expressed in the Bretton Woods Agreement, establishing the International Monetary Fund and reintroducing a regime of (more or less) stable exchange rates after World War II in place of the regime of unstable, fluctuating exchange rates of the 1930's. The agreement pledges all participating nations to the maintenance of full employment.

International trade

Under the international gold standard "there was no means open to a government whereby to mitigate economic distress at home except through the competitive struggle for markets" (382). While paying lip service to the idea that the sole purpose of exporting is to be able to import, all nations, when they suffer from instability and unemployment, try to export as much, and to import as little, as possible. "International trade . . . is . . . a desperate expedient to maintain employment at home by forcing sales on foreign markets and restricting purchases, which, if successful, will merely shift the problem of unemployment to the neighbour . . ." (382-83).

From its own point of view, of course, each nation is justified in trying to maintain domestic employment in this way. The objection that this violates the principle of international division of labor, according to which each nation must produce only goods which it can produce at a lower comparative cost, is not valid. It is better to employ labor in producing goods at home which could be produced more cheaply (i.e., with less labor) abroad, if the alternative is not to employ this labor at all. Keynes added the "unemployment" argument to Adam Smith's "defense" argument and Friedrich List's "infant industries" argument in favor of protectionism. Even as it may be reasonable to restrict international trade if such restriction helps a country to strengthen its defenses, or to develop its infant industries, so it may be reasonable to restrict international trade in order to increase or protect employment at home, though this may cause unemployment abroad.

Notwithstanding his recognition of the advantage to be gained from trade restrictions, Keynes did not advocate them for fear that "private interest, administrative incompetence and the intrinsic difficulty of the task" might produce undesirable results (339). Instead he argued for the measures to produce the conditions of full employment which would make it possible for international trade to be "a willing and unimpeded exchange of goods and services in conditions of mutual advantage" (383).

Chapter Twenty

Evaluation and Criticism of the General Theory

The place and significance of the *General Theory* in economic thought have been commented on in several chapters of this book, particularly Chapters I and XVIII. The present chapter brings together what has already been said elsewhere in the book by way of evaluating and criticizing the *General Theory*, but also introduces some additional thoughts on this subject.

EVALUATION OF THE GENERAL THEORY

The *General Theory* is often ranked with Adam Smith's *Wealth of Nations* and Karl Marx's *Capital* as having greatly influenced economic thinking.[1] The impact of the *General Theory* was unquestionably great. Yet, although the most recent of these three works, it is probably the least read. Whereas both the *Wealth of Nations* and *Capital* have been published in many editions, the *General Theory* has had only one edition so far in the United States.

Smith, the Mercantilists, and Keynes

Adam Smith exposed the fallacies of the mercantilistic doctrines current in his day. These doctrines called for direction and control of economic activities by the state. The need for such state direction and control was, in fact, regarded as a self-evident necessity at that time. Against this mercantilistic in-

---

1. E.g., Slichter, "The Passing of the Keynesian Economics," *Atlantic Monthly*, November, 1957.

terventionism Smith proclaimed the principle of economic free-
dom, or *laissez faire*, based on the doctrine of the "harmony of
interests" which assured that individuals in pursuit of their self-
interest would always unwittingly promote the welfare of the
entire society.

Keynes, in turn, exposed the fallacies of *laissez faire* and the
"harmony of interest." As he saw it, the economy, left to itself,
would produce instability and unemployment. To avoid this,
he preached anew the need for state intervention in the
economy.

In a sense, then, Keynes revived mercantilistic doctrines. He
was aware of this and in fact proclaimed his kinship with the
mercantilists. He paid tribute to their wisdom and insight. He
saw in their theory of money and interest an early version of
his own theory. He said, for instance, that the mercantilists
advocated a "favorable" balance of trade because they saw
that this would lead to the importation of specie—gold and
silver; that this would add to the quantity of media of payments;
that the enlarged quantity of media of payment would drive
down the rate of interest; and that a lower rate of interest would
stimulate investment.

While there are many similarities between Keynesian and
mercantilistic doctrines, there are of course also differences.
Chief among these are the aims and points of departure. The
mercantilists took as their point of departure the national
interest. The greater power, glory, and wealth of the nation
was their aim. The question was how the economy could best
be developed and regulated to serve the interests of the state,
or of the ruler who was practically identified with the state.
Keynes, on the other hand, made the better functioning of the
economy his starting point. For him the question was how the
state could be of service to the economy.

Keynes and Marx

Karl Marx, too, rejected Smith's optimistic "harmony of interests." He argued that capitalism generates class conflicts and
contradictions which would ultimately destroy the capitalistic

system. In several respects, the *General Theory* resembles the theory of Marx. Keynes echoed Marx especially is asserting that:

1. Labor is the only factor of production.
2. To continue to function, the capitalistic system requires an increasingly higher rate of investment.
3. The capitalistic system generates unemployment. (Marx called it the "Industrial Reserve Army.")
4. Capitalism is headed for a permanent crisis within one or two generations.
5. Social direction must replace private direction of economic activities.

While there are similarities, there are of course also many differences between the theories of Marx and Keynes. Keynes disregarded class conflict; he saw no inherent contradictions in the capitalistic mode of production; he assumed that the crisis of capitalism could be resolved and capitalism go on indefinitely, if only effective demand were kept sufficiently high. Even so, his leanings toward Marxian ideas are evident. In *An Essay on Marxian Economics,* Joan Robinson concluded that the Keynesian theory is closer to that of Marx than it is to classical economic theory; she implied that Marx was really a Keynesian.

Keynes himself seems to have been unaware of the resemblance of his ideas to those of Marx. As a staunch defender of capitalism, Keynes had nothing but scorn and disdain for Marx and his works.[2] He regarded Marx as a crackpot or charlatan, on a level with Silvio Gesell and Major Douglas. In fact, he ranked Marx even lower than these propounders of monetary schemes to make capitalism work, especially Gesell. Keynes asserted that "the future will learn more from the spirit of Gesell than from that of Marx"(355).

The General Theory and traditional economics

Although Keynes himself regarded the *General Theory* as the work which would give the death blow to classical economics,

2. It is possible that Keynes had not read the works of Marx. We have it on Harrod's authority that Keynes had not read widely in economics. He seemed to have had a special aversion to German works.

the *General Theory* retains many features of the classical economics. The central concept, around which the *General Theory* is built, is the concept of equilibrium, which is also the pivotal concept of classical economics. Keynes also accepted the marginal analysis, as well as the classical theories of distribution and resource allocation. In fact, Keynes did not challenge the classical theory in most of its essentials. On the contrary, he certified it as completely valid for the situation which the classical economists assumed to prevail always: the situation of full employment. The classical theory, said Keynes, was not wrong; it only needed to be expanded and adjusted to include situations of less than full employment due to insufficiency of effective demand. Keynes did not cut down the tree of classical economics to make way for a new growth, but merely grafted a new theory of aggregate demand onto the old tree.

Keynes's theory firmly established

Twenty years ago disputations about Keynesian economics were often reminiscent of the acrimonious debates about Richard Wagner's music which disturbed the peace of European coffee houses a century ago, when Wagner's music was new. Today the debates about Keynes, like the controversies about Wagner, have largely subsided. Most economists nowadays are neither pro-Keynesian nor anti-Keynesian; but they are definitely not *pre*-Keynesian.[3] The essential contributions of Keynes have been accepted and firmly imbedded in the corpus of contemporary economic theory.

CRITICISMS OF THE GENERAL THEORY

A voluminous literature has grown around the *General Theory*. Every feature of it has been written about; scarcely a line of it has escaped criticism. It would be impossible to mention all the criticisms of the *General Theory* that have been brought forward. But a few of them are listed below. These criticisms of the

3. Cf. Hart, *Money, Debt, and Economic Activity,* p. xi.

General Theory are classified as pertaining to a) its limited applicability, b) its assumptions, c) omissions, d) contradictions contained in it.

Limited applicability of the General Theory

1. The *General Theory* is essentially a "depression theory." Its formulations, and the policies based on them, apply chiefly to situations in which there is unemployment due to insufficient effective demand. In prosperity, such as has prevailed in most capitalistic countries since the end of World War II, the Keynesian theory loses its point, since it is no longer unemployment, but the danger of inflation, which poses the real problem.

This criticism, however, overlooks that the Keynesian theory also has an important bearing on inflation. (See Chapters XIX, p. 183, and XXI, pp. 203-6.)

2. The *General Theory* applies only to industrially advanced capitalistic countries. It is only there that the problem of unemployment due to a deficiency of effective demand is likely to arise, as Keynes himself pointed out. But the great economic problem of the capitalistic world today is not how to fight depression unemployment in developed countries; the problem is how to promote the industrialization of "underdeveloped" countries. The underdeveloped countries also suffer from unemployment, but it is "structural" unemployment, arising from the lack of productive facilities, not depression unemployment, that plagues them. The Keynesian theory throws no light on structural unemployment and how to overcome it.

3. The *General Theory* is a short-run theory which ignores most of the long-run problems and trends. For instance, it treats investment solely from the point of view of the role it plays as a determinant of the community's current income, output and employment; it completely neglects the long-run effects of investment as a claim to future consumption expenditures needed to absorb the consumers' goods produced by the newly created capital, and as a claim to future labor to operate the newly created capital equipment. Also neglected is the role of inventions in creating new investment opportunities.

4. The *General Theory* analyzes only the behavior of aggregates, such as aggregate demand, aggregate consumption and aggregate investment. It neglects important relationships within these aggregates and hides problems arising from changes within aggregates. Relative price changes, for instance, may occasionally be of greater significance than changes in the general price level.

All these criticisms of the *General Theory* for its limited applicability really amount to nothing more than to finding fault with the problems Keynes chose to deal with. But there is rarely any point in quarreling with an author or a scientist for giving his attention to one problem instead of to another. It must have seemed to Keynes that the problems he chose to deal with were important, and it is hard to deny that they were, and continue to be, important. Of course we also want to deal with problems of over-full employment, with problems of economic development, with long-run problems, and with microeconomic problems. That Keynes did not deal with these problems does not seem to be a meaningful criticism of his work.

Assumptions of the General Theory

Keynes accepted all the assumptions of the classical economics, except the "full employment" assumption. In other words, he rejected only the assumption that aggregate demand is always high enough to assure full employment. Criticism of Keynes's assumptions, therefore, must be much the same as criticisms made of the assumptions of classical economics. A few of these criticisms are listed below:

1. The *General Theory* is a highly artificial "model." Keynes assumed certain motives—"the psychological propensity to consume, the psychological attitude to liquidity and the psychological expectation of future yield from capital-assets" (247)— and from these motives deduced the behavior of the economy It is remarkable that the most influential work in economics in the twentieth century (so far) should show so little the effects of the criticism that had long been leveled against this method of analysis. Historical economists and institutional economists

have pleaded for a more scientific, less speculative, approach.[4] They have studied what actually happens in the economy and from these factual studies have tried to reach conclusions regarding the motives and behavior of people. Keynes seems never to have had any doubts about the superiority of the model-building method.

2. The *General Theory* is based on the assumption that "pure" competition prevails. Keynes ignored the role of monopoly. This is remarkable in view of the prominence which "monopolistic competition" theory was achieving at the time Keynes wrote the *General Theory*.

3. Keynes assumed that the private capitalistic system assures optimum allocation of resources. The only thing wrong with the capitalistic system, he said, is that it fails to employ all the workers, not that it misemploys those who are working. "When 9,000,000 men are employed out of 10,000,000 willing and able to work, there is no evidence that the labour of these 9,000,000 men is misdirected. . . . It is in determining the volume, not the direction, of actual employment that the existing system has broken down" (379).

The assumption that the capitalistic system assures the best allocation of resources is questionable. What constitutes the best allocation of resources depends on the goals set for the economy. In war, for instance, resources must be used to achieve victory, and there is no question that this cannot be done except through careful and detailed planning of the use of resources. Free competition could never be relied upon to produce the desired results. Again, if the objective is to abolish poverty and assure more benefits to previously underprivileged people, the use of resources must be centrally planned and directed instead of being left to the free interplay of "market forces." Only if the goal of the economy is to provide for each individual whatever this individual is able to secure for himself in competition with other individuals, then the "free market" system assures the

---

4. On this point, see especially Burns, *Economic Research and the Keynesian Thinking of Our Times*.

best allocation of resources. But this is tautological and meaning-less. It says that whatever is the resource allocation achieved under a "free market" system is the best resource allocation, if that is the kind of resource allocation we want.

4. The *General Theory* assumes that employment fluctuates with output. This assumption no longer fits the facts. The fluctuations in output are much larger than the fluctuations in employment, even in the short run. The reason for this is, partly, that labor unions have won many concessions from employers in making jobs more secure for the workers. Many "employment stabilization" schemes have been written into agreements be-tween employers and unions. Another reason for greater stability of employment than of output is that an increasing proportion of employees are salaried employees who are members of the administrative, research, or technical organizations of firms and who are not "laid off" as easily as factory operatives. Many firms vary their output without significantly varying the number of people they employ.

Omissions in the General Theory

Keynes failed to consider two factors of considerable im-portance in the short-run fluctuations of output and employment: durable consumers' goods and inventories.

In the *General Theory* the aggregate demand for durable consumers' goods—e.g., automobiles—is subsumed under aggre-gate demand for all consumers' goods, C. It will be remembered that Keynes assumed C to be stable in the short run. This assumption, however, is valid only with respect to aggregate demand for nondurable consumers' goods. Aggregate demand for durable consumers' goods is subject to considerable short-run fluctuations. Total expenditures on durable consumers' goods consequently play a role quite similar to that assigned by Keynes exclusively to investment as a determinant of employment.

The omission of the role of inventories hides the important difference between intended and unintended investment.[5] In-vestment can take two forms: it may take the form of additions

5. See Chapter VII, pp. 62-66.

to "capital equipment" (buildings, machinery) or of additions to inventories. Keynes assumed that investment always means additions to "capital equipment." Such investment can take place only if it is intended; and changes in the volume of such investment are due primarily to changes in the marginal efficiency of capital, according to Keynes. Investment in inventories, on the other hand, may be intended or unintended. Changes in the volume of inventory investment are often the result of wrong estimates of what consumers would spend. If goods are left unsold, inventories rise; if consumers spend more than firms expected them to spend, inventories decrease. These unintended changes in inventories, then, are not due to changes in the "marginal efficiency" of capital, but to wrong estimates of effective demand. And it is this type of investment—unintended inventory investment—which is particularly volatile. Unintended changes in inventories set off cyclical fluctuations. Many a boom is an "inventory boom," in which additional production goes largely into swelling inventories; and many a recession is an "inventory recession," due to the decisions of firms to cut down production until excessive inventories are reduced to levels considered "normal."

The omission of durable consumers' goods and of inventories from consideration in the *General Theory* is an example of how the analysis of aggregates—"macro-economics"—can be vitiated by the fact that important differences within the aggregates remain hidden, even as the findings of "micro-economics" were vitiated by failure to consider economic aggregates.[6]

Inaccuracies and contradictions in the General Theory

Every author has the right to choose and limit his subject as he pleases; and he has a right to make assumptions as he pleases. He has no obligations to anyone in these matters. But every author has one duty to his readers and this is to present what he has to say clearly and intelligibly. Keynes did not live up to this obligation; his *General Theory* is full of contradictions and inaccuracies; he did not stick to definitions and terminology

6. See Chapter XVIII, pp. 169-70.

chosen by himself; he shifted his assumptions without indicating this to the reader and probably without being aware of it himself. The result is that the *General Theory* is difficult to understand.

Keynes was a man of many ideas and he was impatient to put his ideas before his fellow economists and before the public as soon as he conceived them and often without giving them time to ripen. In this he was at opposite poles from his teacher Alfred Marshall, who was reluctant to publish anything until he had satisfied himself that he had thought through his problems thoroughly and left no contradictions or loose ends to confuse the reader. Marshall spent twenty years preparing his *Principles of Economics*. Keynes probably spent no more than three years in writing the *General Theory* and revising it in response to criticisms from friends and colleagues, and all this time he was busy with a thousand and one other things besides. No wonder that the *General Theory* is not as smooth a finished piece of work as is Marshall's *Principles*.

The most serious confusions and contradictions of the *General Theory* are found in the theory of aggregate demand and in the theory of interest. Criticisms and more intelligible reformulations of these theories were presented in Chapters IX and XVI of this book. Other instances in which the *General Theory* is unclear or contradictory were also mentioned.

Of course the lack of clarity and precision in the *General Theory* is one main reason why it has been written about so much and is being read so little. If the *General Theory* were intelligible, students of Keynesian economics would turn to it as the original source instead of turning to guides, commentaries, and interpretations. By contrast, students of Marshall's economics even today could not possibly do better than to turn to the *Principles*, where they find the clearest and most systematic exposition of Marshall's theories.

But with all the deficiences of the *General Theory*, Keynes still put across his fundamental and important proposition: that the volume of employment depends on aggregate demand; and that aggregate demand, in most situations, is not sufficient to assure employment to all who are willing to work at prevailing wages.

Chapter Twenty-one

The Principal Works of Keynes

The *General Theory*, with which most of this book is concerned, is the work in which Keynes developed and presented what has come to be known as the Keynesian theory of economics. But it is by no means the only thing he wrote. Keynes was a prolific writer. In addition to the several major economic works briefly discussed in this chapter, he wrote numerous pamphlets and articles in economic journals, magazines, and newspapers. The list of his writing is a long one.[1] In addition to those that were published under his own name there are a number of items written in collaboration with others and some that were published anonymously. Among the last are parliamentary and other official reports which Keynes helped to write, such as the *Report on British Finance and Industry* (Macmillan Report) of 1931. Keynes also wrote on subjects other than economics. One of his books is *A Treatise on Probability*; another is entitled *Essays in Biography*; several articles deal with political and other topics.

INDIAN CURRENCY AND FINANCE

Keynes's first book, on *Indian Currency and Finance,* was published in 1913. Keynes had served two years in the India Office which was directly concerned with problems of the Indian currency. But interest in the question was not limited to officials of the India Office. The Indian currency problem had been discussed and debated by economists in England and elsewhere

1. A list of Keynes's writings appears in Harris, *The New Economics,* pp. 665-86.

ever since 1873. Keynes had written some articles and reviews on the subject before writing his book.

Up to 1873, the currencies of "gold standard" countries (e.g., England) had been linked to those of "silver standard" countries (e.g., Germany, India and most of Asia) through the action of "bimetallic standard" countries (principally France and the United States). In gold standard countries media of payment were convertible at legally fixed rates into gold, in silver standard countries into silver, but in bimetallic countries into both metals, gold or silver. As long as bimetallism existed, therefore, the mutual exchangeability of gold and silver currencies at practically fixed rates was assured.

In 1873, France (and the countries associated with France in the Latin Monetary Union) and the United States abandoned bimetallism for a gold standard and Germany switched from silver to gold. The price of silver dropped. The exchange rate between pound sterling and the Indian rupee was no longer stable and became increasingly unfavorable to India. Several commissions considered the question whether a gold standard should be adopted by India. Still—or again—pursuing this question in 1909, the India Office sought the opinions of Alfred Marshall and Keynes. Keynes detailed his views in *Indian Currency and Finance*. He favored a "gold exchange standard" (i.e., convertibility of the rupee not into gold but into pound sterling exchange) and the establishment of a central bank to manage this gold exchange standard. Already in this book Keynes implied that the gold standard should be abolished entirely and everywhere, a proposal which he later set forth more specifically. He recognized that what mattered in the gold standard was not the convertibility of media of payment into gold, but into media of payment of other countries. It was not a question of tying the "value of money" to that of gold, but of preserving exchange rate stability.

Even before this book was published, Keynes was made a member of a new Commission on Indian Currency and Finance which largely followed his views. This first major appointment established Keynes's reputation as one of the leading economists in England at the time.

THE ECONOMIC CONSEQUENCES OF THE PEACE

The book that made Keynes really famous was *The Economic Consequences of the Peace*. It appeared in 1919, a few months after Keynes had resigned as head of the British Finance Delegation to the Peace Conference of Paris. The book exposes the fraud, the ignorance, meanness, and vindictiveness actuating the framers of the Versailles Treaty, which was couched in high-sounding phrases of justice and morality.

The "Big Four," said Keynes, were not concerned with the problems of Europe, but pursued selfish, petty interests. Clemenceau clamored for revenge; Lloyd George, preoccupied with re-election, promised his electorate to "squeeze the German orange till the pips squeak"; Wilson, giving his consent to the worst depredations, insisted only on the semblance of justice and morality. The incisive personality sketches and the disclosures of behind-the-scenes finagling added much to the popularity of this book.

But the *Consequences* deals primarily with economics. Europe was falling apart, production was low, inflation rampant. Government control of prices was unsuccessful. Inflation had to be stopped, lest Lenin's prophecy that inflation would ruin capitalism come true. Public opinion blamed war profiteers for high prices. But, as Keynes pointed out, war profiteers were simply business people who profited from rising prices; they were not responsible for rising prices. To accuse them endangered the prestige of the business system and the foundations of capitalism.

At the heart of Europe and of Europe's economic problems was Germany. Keynes argued that Germany must regain economic health and prosperity if Europe was to prosper. But German economic recovery was jeopardized by the peace treaty which threatened to crush Germany with impossibly heavy financial burdens. An early British proposal had set the amount of "reparations" which Germany was to pay at 24 billion pound sterling. Keynes had argued that 2 billion pounds was the largest sum feasible. The German reparations debt was eventually fixed at 33 billion dollars.

In *The Economic Consequences of the Peace* Keynes proposed:

1. Revision of the peace treaty. Reparations to be fixed at 50 million pounds a year for 30 years.
2. Cancellation of inter-allied debts.
3. An international loan of 400 million pound sterling to Germany.

Subsequent events largely confirmed the views and prophecies expressed in the *Consequences,* and, in the end, Keynes's recommendations had to be followed. Reparations were eventually scaled down, inter-allied debts were left unpaid, and an international loan was made to Germany. But instead of being put into effect at once and generously, when they could have invigorated the European economy, these measures came as a result of the collapse of that economy, after events had demonstrated the folly of the peace treaty.

For Keynes, *The Economic Consequences of the Peace* was a triumph. The work was widely acclaimed and Keynes's position as a leading economist further secured.

A TRACT ON MONETARY REFORM

The period following World War I was one of currency deterioration. Many parts of the world suffered inflation in various degrees. Prices rose, exchange rates were unstable. Restoration of monetary stability was a main object of economic policy and subject of economic discussion. Return to the gold standard seemed to most economists and policy makers to assure monetary stability.

Keynes set forth his views on this question in *A Tract on Monetary Reform,* published in 1923. Already in *Indian Currency and Finance* he had espoused the idea of a "managed currency." Now he elaborated the idea further. The question, as he saw it, was not whether or not to have a managed currency, but to what purpose the currency should be managed. There are two possible objectives, he said: price level stability or exchange rate stability Keynes argued the case for price level stability. The gold standard, he contended, could not assure stability of the price level because the quantity of gold would not increase sufficiently to keep pace with economic expansion and the resulting increase in the demand for media of payment.

With the aid of a new equation of exchange (see Chapter XVII, p. 156) which Keynes developed in this book, he showed that the central bank can regulate the amount of reserves held by commercial banks and the amount of media of payment held by the public in such a way as to offset any changes in the demand for "cash balances." In this manner, he argued, price level stability can be assured.

A TREATISE ON MONEY

In 1930, Keynes's two-volume work *A Treatise on Money* was published. The largest of his works, it is, in the opinion of his biographer, Sir Roy Harrod, also the most important and characteristic. The main ideas of the "Keynesian system" are to be found here, some of them more carefully elaborated than in the *General Theory*. In the *Treatise*, however, Keynes had not yet developed the analytical framework and the terminology which he employed in presenting these ideas in the *General Theory*.

If the difference between the *Treatise* and the *General Theory* is chiefly in the method of formulating ideas, the difference between the *Treatise* and the *Tract* is more in the ideas themselves. In the *Treatise* Keynes developed a new theory of price level determinants. He formulated this theory in a series of equations, one of which was briefly discussed in Chapter XVII, (pp. 157-58). The dominant new idea in the *Treatise* is that the price level is not regulated by the quantity of media of payment, but by the relation between saving and investment. This idea, which dominated Keynesian thought henceforward, was totally absent in his earlier work.

Keynes seems to have been led to a recognition of the importance of saving and investment in the course of discussions with his Cambridge colleague Dennis H. Robertson, who in his book *Banking Policy and the Price Level* (1926) analyzed the connection between saving and investment and prices. Robertson had not been the first to discover this connection. A quarter of a century earlier the Swedish economist Knut Wicksell, in his *Geldzins und Güterpreise,* published in German in 1898, had called attention to saving and investment as determinants of the price level. Keynes adopted Wicksell's analysis in the *Treatise.* Keynes argued that the amounts saved are not equal to the amounts invested, except in equilibrium. The divergence of saving from investment is to be expected since the people who invest are not the same as the people who save. Investments are made by entrepreneurs, by business firms, by the dispensers of income; saving, on the other hand, is done by the recipients of income. When saving exceeds investment, prices fall; when investment exceeds saving, prices rise.

The volume of investment is influenced by the rate of interest; and the rate of interest is significant primarily as a determinant of investment. The task of the central bank is to manipulate Bank-rate in order to influence investment in such a way as to make the general price level rise or fall or remain stable, as the objectives of policy may dictate.

Keynes had not as yet clearly crystallized the concept of the propensity to save (or rather its inverse, the propensity to consume) as distinguished from actual saving (or consumption). His argument ran in terms of deviations of actual saving from actual investment, rather than in terms of deviations of intended saving from intended investment, as in the *General Theory,* where actual, realized, saving is by definition always equal to actual investment. As was pointed out in Chapter XII, the equality or inequality of actual saving and actual investment depends on definitions of saving and investment. In the *Treatise,* Keynes defined saving as including only saving out of factor incomes—wages, rent, interest—and normal profit,[2] but excluding saving out of windfall profit. (Windfall profit or loss is the difference between the normal profit and the profit actually realized by the firm.) Saving so defined is not necessarily equal to investment. When saving out of factor incomes and normal profit is less than investment, the difference accrues to firms as windfall profits; when saving exceeds investment, firms suffer losses. The windfall profits or losses added to saving out of factor

2. See Chapter II, p. 25.

incomes and normal profit always yield a figure exactly equal to investment. In other words, total saving (including windfall profit) always equals investment.

The reason why Keynes excluded windfall profit from his definitions of income and saving in the *Treatise* was that he regarded windfall profits or losses as the dynamic element in economic fluctuations. He wanted to set apart this dynamic element from other incomes; and to show how windfall profit or loss depend on the relation between the volume of investment and the amounts saved out of factor incomes and normal profit.

Shortcomings of the *Treatise,* corrected by Keynes in the *General Theory,* are that:

1. As pointed out above, it does not clearly formulate the concept of the propensity to consume and the consumption function.
2. It centers on explanations of price levels rather than income and employment.
3. It puts too much reliance on the monetary system as "central controls of our economic life" and fails to recognize the need for more direct intervention by the state to regulate consumption and investment.

HOW TO PAY FOR THE WAR

In the process of writing the *Treatise* Keynes had already transcended some of the more traditional views he had held before he embarked on that work. The final reformulation of his ideas appeared in 1936, in the *General Theory.* From that time onward until the outbreak of World War II in 1939, Keynes was engaged primarily in defending, elaborating, and amending the *General Theory.* A severe illness restricted his creative activities.

The outbreak of war occasioned publication, in 1940, of another book by Keynes: *How to Pay for the War.* It was a short book and his last. During the war and until his death in 1946, Keynes devoted his energies mainly to his work as economic adviser to the British government and as its chief representative at international conferences dealing with economic and financial matters.

In *How to Pay for the War* Keynes applied the principles of the *General Theory* to the war situation. He showed that his theory was relevant not only to depression and unemployment, but also to over-full employment and inflationary situations.

There are three ways to pay for the war, said Keynes: taxation, inflation, and "compulsory saving." Keynes's scheme was compulsory saving. This he proposed as a more equitable way of financing war than had been followed in past wars. The expenses of World War I, for instance, had been covered in large part by borrowing. But since people were not willing to save enough to buy the securities offered by the government, these securities were sold to the banks which bought them with media of payment newly created for that purpose. This was inflationary. The government demand for goods added to that of consumers who would not retrench their expenditures drove prices up. Rising prices resulted in larger profits for capitalists and lower real wages for workers.

Keynes proposed that World War II expenditures, in so far as they were not covered by taxes, should be financed by borrowing, not from banks, but from the public. This would be non-inflationary because increased government expenditures would be counterbalanced by reduced consumer expenditures. If consumers were not willing to curtail their expenditures and thus save enough to supply the government with the needed media of payment, they should be compelled to save. This could be done by withholding a part of the worker's pay from his pay envelope in the same way that taxes are withheld. Instead of being simply taken away from the wage earner, however, these compulsory savings would be credited to him and be available to him after the war and would therefore be in the nature of "deferred pay" rather than of a tax. Through such compulsory saving prices of goods could be kept from rising. The future purchasing power of the savings would be preserved. At the end of the war it would be not the capitalists but the consumers themselves who would have something to show for the sacrifices they made during the war.

A new concept introduced by Keynes in this last of his books is the "inflationary gap," briefly discussed in Chapter XIX, page 183, above. The problem, in the war, was to close the inflationary gap by cutting down private expenditures. This was the only way to avoid inflation. Questions of finance and of the "quantity of money" were secondary.

BASIC IDEAS RUNNING THROUGH
KEYNES'S ECONOMIC WORKS

There is a continuity of basic ideas running through all of Keynes's economic works and giving them unity and character. These basic ideas may be summarized as follows:

1. Capitalism is good and should be preserved.
2. Two weaknesses threaten the continued existence of capitalism: instability and unemployment.
3. The state must intervene to remedy these weaknesses and thus to save capitalism.
4. The state should restrict its intervention to regulating aggregate demand and to managing the monetary system. The rest of the economy should be left to itself.
5. Economic difficulties are due to bad arrangements (e.g., the gold standard), not to the basic structure of society. Difficulties can be overcome or removed by improving the arrangements, by introducing this or that "scheme"—a gold exchange standard, a central bank, compulsory saving, etc.[3]
6. In the last analysis, all capitalistic troubles can be cured with one remedy: money. Until the end of his life Keynes championed monetary schemes. Though his faith in money suffered a setback in the *General Theory*, even this work, as all his other economic writings, revolved importantly

---

3. Keynes's propensity for "schemes" had earned him the nickname of "Pozzo" among his Bloomsbury friends. Harrod explained that Pozzo was a Corsican diplomat—"not a diplomat of evil motive or base conduct, but certainly a schemer and a man of many facets" (*Life of John Maynard Keynes*, p. 180). Clive Bell wrote that "Pozzo was a pet name for Maynard which Maynard particularly disliked" (*Old Friends*, p. 134). But Maynard's friends must have thought it highly fitting.

around the idea that monetary manipulation could solve economic problems. Keynes's last achievements were his part in the establishment of an International Bank and International Monetary Fund, and the four billion dollar American loan to England—more monetary and financial schemes to restore the world to economic health.

7. The purpose and aim of Keynes's economic writings are, in the first place, to win support for some policy or scheme. Only in the second place are they concerned with scientific analysis. His theories mainly serve to supply the arguments in favor of the proposed schemes and policies.

Chapter Twenty-two

Life and Character of
John Maynard Keynes

A brief biographical and character sketch of Keynes is presented here with the thought that to know something of the life, environment, interests, and activities of a man helps to understand what he thought and taught.

The information used in this chapter is derived from several sources, chiefly from *The Life of John Maynard Keynes* by Sir Roy F. Harrod, the only full-length biography of Keynes published to date; and from an extensive memoir of Keynes by E. A. G. Robinson in *The Economic Journal* of March, 1947. More intimate character sketches of Keynes are drawn by Clive Bell in *Old Friends* and by David Garnett in *The Flowers of the Forest*. All these authors knew Keynes well and their reports may be trusted.

FAMILY BACKGROUND

John Maynard Keynes, called Maynard, belonged to a thoroughly English family which epitomized the prosperous, solid, and conservative Victorian Age. His father, John Neville Keynes, also a noted economist (*The Scope and Method of Political Economy*, 1891), was a well-known figure in Cambridge. Grandfather Keynes had been a manufacturer who apparently left enough wealth to enable the family to enjoy a life of comfort and security in an ample house well staffed with servants.

Maynard's mother was the daughter of the Reverend Dr. Brown, a protestant divine, historian, and writer. She too was an eminent person, well known in her community for her social welfare activities and other social and political interests. Among other things she was mayor of Cambridge. Both his parents outlived Maynard.

Maynard Keynes was interested in genealogy and he was proud of his ancestors. According to his own report, his family can be traced back to a William de Cahagnes who lived at the time of William the Conqueror. Later ancestors, too, were prominent people. One of them had owned Tilton, the country seat which Maynard eventually bought and from which he derived his predicate, Baron Tilton. (He was made a lord in 1942).

In addition to counting aristocrats among its ancestors, the Keynes family was related, in Maynard's own time, to families whose names are famous in science. His brother married a granddaughter of Charles Darwin. His sister married the physiologist A. V. Hill, who won the Nobel prize in 1922. One of Maynard's nephews married the daughter of another Nobel laureate, the physiologist E. A. Adrian.

EDUCATION

Eton College was almost as a matter of course the school to which Keynes was sent. It was the school for boys of his class. At Eton many of his schoolmates were sons of influential families, people who by and from birth were destined for leading positions. The atmosphere of such a school naturally tends to further the self-confidence and self-esteem of the students, to give them a feeling of superiority, of belonging to an elite of English gentlemen. At least this is what it seems to have done for Maynard Keynes.

From Eton, Keynes went to King's College in Cambridge. There he was again among the elite, for here, too, many of the students were people who later distinguished themselves in science, in literature, in politics. In his first years at Cambridge, Keynes devoted himself chiefly to the study of mathematics.

Cambridge must have been an extraordinarily stimulating place at the time Keynes studied there. There was a universality and diversity of interests which students could pursue such as is unknown to students at most present-day American universities. There was little emphasis on specialization and on lectures. Cambridge students were in close touch with professors and dons. Keynes learned economics not only in lectures, but probably even more at his weekly breakfasts with A. C. Pigou, Marshall's protégé and eventual successor. In 1904 Keynes was the sole student attending a lecture course by Alfred N. Whitehead. (Whitehead, a famous philosopher who later taught at Harvard, declared Keynes to have been one of his most gifted students.) There were many discussion groups in which Cambridge luminaries participated. Keynes was a zealous and much sought-after member of several such groups. In a memoir entitled *My Early Beliefs*[1] Keynes told about the subjects discussed in these Cambridge circles during his student days and about the views held by himself and his friends. These views, Keynes wrote, were Utopian, melioristic, and rationalistic. He might have added that they were also conservative. Although in the memoir Keynes smiled over his early beliefs, yet they continued in large measures to be the beliefs he held in later life. Throughout his life Keynes was a meliorist; a world reformer; a rationalist who, in the face of discouraging evidence, continued to trust in human reason; and a conservative who wanted to preserve the social order as he found it in his youth.

Another trait of the Cambridge circles to which Keynes belonged seems to have been a certain exclusiveness and presumptuousness. An incident told by Harrod illustrates this attitude. Harrod had been in Cambridge a short time when he asked people he had met to introduce him to some others, as he wanted to know all sides of Cambridge life. The response he got was "But there isn't anyone else."[2] Perhaps this idea that "there isn't anyone else" is, or was, characteristic of all Cambridge; perhaps only of King's College. Certainly it expressed the attitude of Keynes about Cambridge economists, of whom he became the most famous. In his view, they were the best in the world; there was nothing worth-while in economics outside of Cambridge. Keynes paid little attention to any economists

1. Keynes, *Two Memoirs.*
2. Harrod, *The Life of John Maynard Keynes,* p. 322.

who did not think and write along the lines of the "Cambridge school." The contributions of German economists he dismissed with the remark that he had never got any new idea from them. He did not read widely in economics and apparently knew little of the works of the American institutionalists—Thorstein Veblen, Wesley C. Mitchell, J. R. Commons, John M. Clark—although they had anticipated some of his own thoughts. But perhaps he would have found nothing new in them either. Keynes's controversies were primarily with other Cambridge economists. Cambridge, as he said, was the only place where they knew anything about economics. There was no other place, not even in England.

THE BLOOMSBURY SET

After he finished his studies in Cambridge, Keynes spent much of his time in London. There he was a member of the circle known as the Bloomsbury set, so named after the section of London where the life of this group centered. Prominent in the Bloomsbury set were Virginia Woolf and her sister Vanessa Bell, Lytton Strachey, Duncan Grant, E. M. Forster, Leonard Woolf, Roger Fry—all well-known artists or writers. The members of this set have been described as affected, conceited people, concerned only with the successes of their own coterie, contemptuous of outsiders, cultivating a distinctive voice and manner of speech, imitating the cadence and peculiar pronunciation of Lytton Strachey, and making fun of other people. "Maynard's sparkling spirits and his impishness made their contribution," Harrod wrote. "He might go forth into the grave world of high finance and politics; but he came back full of stories of how ludicrously and comically people were behaving, often parodying them, and exaggerating shamelessly."[3]

The first headquarters of the Bloomsbury Group was the house at No. 46 Gordon Square which Keynes later bought and which was his London residence from 1916 until his death. In this Bloomsbury set Keynes apparently felt at home. Here he was in the world of literature, of art, and of the theater which

3. *Ibid.*, p. 184.

he loved. Here he met Lydia Lopokova, the Russian dancer and actress whom he married in 1925.

AN ELITE MAN

Wherever Keynes was, there, so to speak, was the center of the world, or rather its summit. And wherever Keynes was, there he stood on the summit. He was always of the elite. As a student at Eton and Cambridge he was immediately recognized as an important person, a leader. When he began to study economics, he was at once one of the chosen few. Marshall, his teacher and the Nestor of economics, recognized Keynes's excellence and gave him his first teaching appointment. As a teacher, again, he was at the top from the beginning—at the leading university, Cambridge, "the only place where they knew anything about economics."[4]

When he was twenty-eight years old, Keynes became the editor of *The Economic Journal*. He had never before edited a scientific journal and had written only a few articles. Yet he was entrusted with the guidance, not of a more modest publication at first, but of the world's foremost economic journal.

Also in government service Keynes was among the elite from the beginning. Already in World War I, at the age of thirty-two years, he was one of the key men in the British Treasury, a friend and frequent guest of the Prime Minister. In World War II, though holding no administrative office or cabinet post, he was the British government's highest adviser on monetary and financial matters.

Keynes was one of those few men who do not have to struggle for their successes, but who achieve them with ease, as a matter of course. He did not have to work his way up; he began at the top and stayed there all his life.

4. Harrod wrote that in his first years of teaching, before World War I, Keynes had certainly gone "through the mill of hard university teaching." Actually Keynes had, from the outset, a schedule which most university teachers regard as a sinecure. The "hard university teaching" consisted in his having to lecture five hours a week. To the American university instructor who usually has to teach twelve hours a week or more, such a teaching load would appear as partial retirement.

INTERESTS AND ACTIVITIES

Keynes was extraordinarily receptive and efficient and had a great capacity for work. These qualities enabled him to pursue many interests and to add new interests and occupations without sacrificing the old. The extensiveness and diversity of his concurrent activities can be seen from the following compilation:

1908–1940 (With interruptions) Lecturer at Cambridge University.

1911–1944 Editor of *The Economic Journal.*

1913–1946 Secretary of the Royal Economic Society. During most of these thirty-three years he also managed the finances of the Society.

1920–1946 Bursar of King's College, Cambridge.

1921–1938 Chairman, National Mutual Life Insurance Company. Also active in several investment firms.

1923–1946 Board member and Chairman of Finance Committee of the Provincial Insurance Company.
Editor of the *Nation,* Board Chairman of the *New Statesman and Nation.*

1925–1946 Managed his estate, Tilton, of some 570 acres.

1932–1936 Treasurer of Camargo Ballet Society.

1935–1938 Founded and managed finances of Cambridge Arts Theater. After 1938 Keynes was a trustee for the theater.

1941–1946 Trustee of National Gallery.
Director of Bank of England.
organized Committee for Encouragement of Music and Arts (CEMA, made a permanent governmental organization in 1945 under the name of Arts Council of Great Britain).

This list does not include all of Keynes's varied interests and activities. His main occupation, after all, was writing. The list of his published writings, as mentioned earlier, is a long one—

244 titles. In addition he was an ardent collector of books and pictures. He also managed his own fortune of approximately $2 million, acquired largely through speculation.

The enormous amount of work which Keynes did is all the more impressive in view of his physical condition. Tall and lanky, he was not robust and was often ill. The last nine years of his life he was an invalid, though even then he continued to work at the pace one would ordinarily expect only from a vigorous man in good health.

Endowed with an outgoing personality and a natural liking for people, Keynes had many friends. Friendship was one of his main interests in life. He was loyal to his friends and put himself out for them. In World War I, for instance, he bought a country place mainly as a refuge where his pacifist friends could perform the farm labor required by law of those who refused military service.

Keynes traveled widely from his youth onward. We find him vacationing, now in France, now in Italy, then again in Egypt or Germany, usually accompanied by friends or staying with friends. He led a sociable life, liked to drink champagne, loved to gamble and play. He was an expert at bridge, played the game for high stakes and usually won. A genial host, he found many occasions for giving parties.

CHARACTERISTICS

Keynes was highly intelligent, quick-witted, often roguish, "a clever economist," as the *London Times* once characterized him. He was a brilliant speaker, teacher, and writer. He had the gift of seeing at once through any problem that came up and of going straight to the central issues. He could shift his thoughts easily from one problem to another.

In his views and tastes Keynes was an aristocrat. He wanted nothing but the best of everything in life. He loved what was true and genuine, he despised the superficial, the slipshod. Also in his political views he was an aristocrat. He identified himself with the upper class; he did not pretend to champion the interests of the lower classes, of the working people, though he displayed toward the latter a typically aristocratic attitude of *noblesse oblige*—of fair play.

Keynes's love for excellence expressed itself also in intolerance of stupidity. His own intelligence being high, he was intolerant of many people—especially of politicians, whom he considered a stupid lot. He was conscious of his superior intelligence and inclined to display it. He was self-assured; some described him as "cocksure." "Cocksureness was his besetting sin." "He laid down the law on all subjects," even those he knew nothing about.[5] One of his friends said he believed "Maynard had a touch of what the French call *folie de grandeur*—an overweening sense of his own importance."[6]

Toward the end of his life he apparently considered himself to be the only man capable of guiding Great Britain's destinies and saving her from destruction. Harrod wrote that shortly before his death Keynes was disturbed by the state of the nation's affairs. "He looked in vain for capable leaders . . . He knew from Dr. Plesch [his physician] that he was in no fit state to run the country. Yet, how otherwise was it to be run?"[7]

5. Bell, *Old Friends,* p. 48.
6. Garnett, *The Flowers of the Forest,* p. 149.
7. Harrod, *op. cit.,* p. 641.

Chronology

1883 Born in Cambridge, England, June 5.

1897 Entered Eton College where he distinguished himself as a scholar, won many prizes.

1902 Entered King's College, Cambridge University, studied mathematics.

1905 Ranked twelfth in mathematics examination; devoted himself to study of Economics, at the urging of Alfred Marshall.

1906 Employed at India Office in London.

1908 Returned to Cambridge as lecturer in Economics.

1909 Elected Fellow of King's College.

1913 Published his first book, on *Indian Currency and Finance*; was made a member of the Royal Commission on Indian Finance and Currency.

1915 Served in high position in British Treasury.

1919 Led British Financial Delegation at Peace Conference in Paris; published *The Economic Consequences of the Peace.*

1919 Resumed his lectures at Cambridge; wrote many pamphlets and articles; speculated successfully, accumulated a fortune of approximately £500,000; became a director of several financial firms and insurance companies.

1925 Married Lydia Lopokova, a Russian dancer and actress.

1929 Member of the Committee of Finance and Industry (Macmillan Committee).

1930 Member of the Economic Advisory Council (to advise the cabinet).

1937 Suffered a severe heart attack from which he never fully recovered.

1940–1946 Member of Consultative Council of the Chancellor of the Exchequer; represented Great Britain at Bretton Woods and other international conferences.

1942 Elevated to nobility, as Baron Keynes of Tilton.

1946 Died of a heart attack at his country house, Tilton, on April 21.

List of Works
Mentioned in This Book

BELL, CLIVE. *Old Friends*. New York: Harcourt Brace and Company, 1957.

BURNS, ARTHUR F. *Economic Research and the Keynesian Thinking of Our Time*. New York: National Bureau of Economic Research, 1946.

COMMITTEE ON FINANCE AND INDUSTRY. *Report*. London: H. M. Stationery Office, 1931 (Macmillan Report).

DILLARD, DUDLEY. *The Economics of John Maynard Keynes*. London: Crosby Lockwood & Son Ltd., 1956. (First published in New York by Prentice-Hall, Inc., 1948.)

GARNETT, DAVID. *The Flowers of the Forest*. New York: Harcourt Brace and Company, 1956.

HANSEN, ALVIN H. *A Guide to Keynes*. New York: McGraw-Hill Book Company, Inc., 1953.

HARRIS, SEYMOUR E. (ed.). *The New Economics*. New York: Alfred A. Knopf, 1950.

HARROD, ROY, F. *The Life of John Maynard Keynes*. London: Macmillan & Co., Ltd., 1952.

HART, ALBERT GAILORD. *Money, Debt, and Economic Activity*. Second edition. New York: Prentice-Hall, Inc., 1953.

HAZLITT, HENRY. *The Failure of the New Economics*. Princeton, New Jersey: Van Nostrand, 1959.

KAHN, R. F. "The Relation of Home Investment to Unemployment," *The Economic Journal*, June 1931.

KEYNES, JOHN MAYNARD. *A Tract on Monetary Reform*. American edition: *Monetary Reform*, New York: Harcourt Brace and Company, 1924.

———. *A Treatise on Money*, 2 vols. New York: Harcourt Brace and Company, 1930.

———. *A Treatise on Probability*. London: Macmillan & Co., Ltd., 1921.

———. *Essays in Biography*. London: Macmillan & Co., Ltd., 1933.

————. *How to Pay for the War*. New York: Harcourt Brace and Company, 1940.

————. *Indian Currency and Finance*. London: Macmillan & Co., Ltd., 1913.

————. *The Economic Consequences of the Peace*. New York: Harcourt Brace and Howe, 1920.

————. *The General Theory of Employment, Interest and Money*. New York: Harcourt Brace and Company, 1936.

————. *Two Memoirs*. London: Rupert Hart-Davis, 1949.

KEYNES, JOHN NEVILLE. *The Scope and Method of Political Economy*. London: Macmillan & Co., Ltd., 1891.

KLEIN, LAWRENCE R. *The Keynesian Revolution*. New York: The Macmillan Company, 1947.

KURIHARA, KENNETH K. *Introduction to Keynesian Dynamics*. New York: Columbia University Press, 1957.

————. (ed.). *Post Keynesian Economics*. New Brunswick, New Jersey: Rutgers University Press, 1954.

————. "Professor Hansen on America's Economic Revolution," *The Economic Journal*, September 1958.

LERNER, ABBA P. "Interest Theory—Supply and Demand for Loans or Supply and Demand for Cash," *The Review of Economics and Statistics*, May 1944. Reprinted in *The New Economics*, edited by Seymour E. Harris. New York: Alfred A. Knopf, 1950.

MARSHALL, ALFRED. *Principles of Economics*. Eighth edition. London: Macmillan & Co., Ltd., 1930. (First published in 1890).

MARX, KARL. *Capital*. Chicago: Charles H. Kerr & Company, 1906. (First published in German in 1867.)

MARX, KARL and ENGELS, FREDERICK. *Communist Manifesto*. Many editions. (First published in German in London: 1848.)

MILL, JOHN STUART. *Principles of Political Economy*. Several editions. (First published in London by Parker & Co., 1848.)

PIGOU, A. C. *Lapses from Full Employment*. London: Macmillan & Co., Ltd., 1945.

————. *Theory of Unemployment*. London: Macmillan & Co., Ltd., 1933.

RICARDO, DAVID. *The Principles of Political Economy and Taxation*. Many editions. (First published in London, 1817.)

ROBERTSON, DENNIS H. *Banking Policy and the Price Level*. Westminster: P. S. King & Son, Ltd., 1926.

ROBINSON, E. A. G. "John Maynard Keynes 1883–1946," *The Economic Journal*, March 1947.

ROBINSON, JOAN. *An Essay on Marxian Economics.* London: Macmillan & Co., Ltd., 1942.

—————. *Introduction to the Theory of Employment.* New York: The Macmillan Company, 1937.

SLICHTER, SUMMER H. "The Passing of Keynesian Economics," *Atlantic Monthly,* November 1957. Reprinted in *The Means to Prosperity.* Buffalo: Economica Books. Smith, Keynes & Marshall, Publishers, 1959.

SMITH, ADAM. *An Inquiry into the Nature and Causes of the Wealth of Nations.* Many editions. (First published in London, 1776.)

Webster's New International Dictionary. 2nd edition. G. & C. Merriam Company, Publishers. Springfield, Mass., 1939.

WICKSELL, KNUT. *Geldzins und Güterpreise,* 1898. English translation: *Interest and Prices.* London: Macmillan & Co., Ltd., 1936.

Index

Abstinence theory of interest, 145
Acceleration effect, 49, 94
Aggregate demand, 23-34, 35, 56, 65-66: defined, 23, 60; objective and subjective, 59-61; schedule, 23
Aggregate demand function, 28-34, 65
Aggregate supply, 23-27
Aggregate supply function, 30, 31
Anti-inflation policy, 183-84
Autonomous investment, 48-49, 94

Bell, Clive, 205n, 207, 214n
Bloomsbury set, 210-11
Bretton Woods Conference, 179, 185
Burns, Arthur F., 193n

Cambridge equation of exchange, 156
Capitalistic system, instability in, 17, 175
Cash balances equation, 155-57
Cash transactions equation, 155
Class character of economics, 15-16
Classical theory of wages and employment, 114-21
Commercial banks: functions of, 106-8; socialization of, 178-79
Compensatory fiscal policy, 182-84
Compulsory saving, 204
Consequences of the Peace, 199-200
Consume, propensity to (see propensity to consume)
Consumption: defined, 36; intended and unintended, 62-66; psychological law of, 40, 68-69, 70; theory of, 35-42
Consumption function, 37-42, 65, 68-77
Consumption ratio, marginal, 84-85
Cournot, Antoine, 14

Currency, how created, 106-8
Cyclical unemployment, 21

D line, 29, 30
Deficit spending, 181-82
Demand, aggregate (see aggregate demand)
Demand, effective, 33, 64, 66, 169
Demand deposit, defined, 107
Demand function, aggregate, 28-34, 65
Demand for labor, 115-16
Demand, insufficiency of, 15-16, 58
Deposit currency, 106-8
Depression policies, 180-83
Depression remedied by public spending, 172
Dillard, Dudley, Preface, 33n, 124n, 154n
Disutility of labor, 116-17
Douglas, Major, 189
Dynamic analysis, 90-91

"Easy money" policy, 180
Economic Consequences of the Peace, 199-200
Economic policies, 175-86: international, 184-86; Keynesian and pre-Keynesian, 184; long-run, 175-79; short-run, 179-84
Economic reforms advocated by Keynes, 176-79
Economics, and economic policy, 16: as ideology, 16-18; as science, 16; class character of, 15-16; national character of, 14
Effective demand, 33, 64, 66, 169; and prices, 162-66
Effective quantity of money, 155
Elasticity of demand, 132n
Employment, determinants of, 20-

27, 67, 117; full, defined, 123; how to increase, 117-18, 122-23

Employment and wages, 114-26, 168-69

Employment multiplier, 92

Entrepreneur, 22n

Equilibrium of saving and investment, 98

Equilibrium output, 26, 34

Euthanasia of the rentier, 79, 177-79

Exchange rate stability, 185

Expectations, 23, 174

Expenditure gap, 50-51, 54-55

Factor costs, 25n

Fallacy of composition, 100, 170

Fiscal policy, 181-84

Frictional unemployment, 21

Full employment, defined, 123

Funds, 106-13

Garnett, David, 207, 214n

General price level, determinants of, 158-64

General Theory, evaluation and criticism of, 187-96

George, Henry, 183

Gesell, Silvio, 189

Gold standard, 186, 200-1

Hansen, Alvin H., Preface, 37n, 46n, 77n, 139n, 148, 148n

Harris, Seymour E., 139n, 197n

Harrod, Roy F., 15n, 18n, 189n, 205n, 207, 209n, 211n, 214n

Hart, Albert Gaylord, 190n

Hazlitt, Henry, Preface

How to Pay for the War, 203-5

Ideology in economics, 16-18

Income, relation to employment and output, 22; falsely identified with money, 160-61

Income line, 39

Indian Currency and Finance, 197-98

Induced investment, 48-49, 94

Industrial Reserve Army, 189

Inflationary gap, 183, 205

Instability in capitalistic system, 17, 175

Interest, abolition of, advocated by Keynes, 176-77; arises from liquidity preference, 172-73; as payment for a service, 146-48; as property income, 146-48; defined, 127, 128; paid for creating liquidity, 143

Interest rate, 45, 47-48; determinants of, 129-37

Interest theory, 127-40; abstinence, 145; criticism of Keynesian, 141-52; Keynesian compared with classical, 137-38; loanable funds, 139-40; reformulation of, 150-52

International Bank, 206

International gold standard, 186

International Monetary Fund, 185, 206

International trade, 186

Investment, autonomous, 48-49, 94; defined, 43; determinants of, 45-48; equal to saving, 97-101; induced, 48-49, 94; instability of, 49-56; intended and unintended, 62-66, 98; theory of, 43-49

Investment and income, 50-55

Investment and saving, 54-55

Investment function, 65

Investment funds, 111-13

Investment multiplier, 92

Kahn, R. F., 91

Keynes, John Maynard: basic ideas of, 205-6; characteristics of, 213-14; chronology of life of, 215-16; education of, 208-10; family background of, 207-8; interests and activities of, 212-13

Keynesian revolution, 18-19, 167-74

Klein, Lawrence R., 18n

Kurihara, Kenneth K., 37n, 62n, 95n, 178, 178n

L function, 129-35, 142-43

Labor, demand for, 115-16; marginal

disutility of, 116-17; supply of, 116-17
Laissez-faire, opposed by Keynes, 18, 188
Leakage, 92-93
Lerner, Abba P., 139, 139n
Liquidity, meaning of, 127; motives for, 128-29
Liquidity preference, 47, 127, 145, 172-73
Liquidity preference function, 129-35, 142-43
Liquidity preference schedule, 129-35, 142-43
Liquidity preference theory, 141-42; apologetic character of, 145-46
List, Friedrich, 14, 183, 186
Loanable funds theory of interest, 139-40
Lopokova, Lydia, 211

Macro-economics, 169
Managed currency, 200
Marginal consumption ratio, 84-85
Marginal efficiency of capital, 45-47
Marginal propensity to consume, 69-70
Marginal saving ratio, 84
Marshall, Alfred, 14, 156, 196, 198
Marx, Karl, 15, 182, 187, 188-89
Media of payment, defined, 47n; demand for, 129-35; effects of changes in quantity of, 159-66; falsely identified with income, 160-61; how created, 106-10; Keynes's view regarding their role, 154-58, 174; supply of, 144-45
Mercantilists, 187-88
Micro-economics, 169
Mill, John Stuart, 14, 146
Monetary policy, 180-81
Monetary theory, integrated with value theory, 170-71; three meanings of, 153-54
Money and prices, theory of, 153-66
Money as a store of value, 173-74
Money, quantity of (see quantity of money; see also media of payment)

Money wage bargains and real wages, 120-21
Money wages, results of cutting, 122, 125-26
Multiplier, 53, 83-95, 99
My Early Beliefs, 209

National character of economics, 14
Normal profit, 25n
Note currency, 106-8

Paradox of thrift, 171-72
Pigou, A. C., 114, 118, 124n, 125
Pigou effect, 124, 125
Policies, economic (see economic policies)
Pozzo, 205n
Price level, determinants of, 158-66, 174
Prices, theory of, 159-66
Propensity to consume, 36-42; average and marginal, 69-70; contrasted with consumption function, 71-72; low in rich countries, 56; stability of, 41-42, 56
Propensity to save, 80; and saving function, 81
Profit, normal, 25n
Protectionism, 186
Psychological law of consumption, 40, 68-69, 70
Public spending as depression remedy, 172
Pump-priming, 182

Quantity of money, and income, 160; effective, 155; effects of changes in, 159-66; relation to investment, 161
Quantity theory of money, 155-57
Quesnay, François, 14

Rate of interest (see interest rate)
Redistribution of income, 176
Reforms advocated by Keynes, 176-79
Rentier, euthanasia of, 79, 177-79